SEPARATE
NO MORE

SEPARATE NO MORE

Understanding and Developing
Racial Reconciliation in Your Church

Norman Anthony Peart

Foreword by John Perkins

BakerBooks

A Division of Baker Book House Co
Grand Rapids, Michigan 49516

© 2000 by Norman Anthony Peart

Published by Baker Books
a division of Baker Book House Company
P.O. Box 6287, Grand Rapids, MI 49516-6287

Printed in the United States of America

Library of Congress Cataloging-in-Publication Data

Peart, Norman Anthony, 1961–
    Separate no more : understanding and developing racial reconciliation in your church / Norman Anthony Peart ; foreword by John Perkins.
        p.   cm.
    Includes bibliographical references.
    ISBN 0-8010-6337-X (paper)
    1. Race relations—Religious aspects—Christianity. 2. Race relations—Biblical teaching. 3. United States—Race relations. I. Title.
BT734.2.P43   2000
261.8'348'00973—dc21   00-039785

Unless otherwise indicated, Scripture quotations are taken from the NEW AMERICAN STANDARD BIBLE ®. Copyright © The Lockman Foundation 1960, 1962, 1963, 1968, 1971, 1972, 1973, 1975, 1977, 1995. Used by permission.

For current information about all releases from Baker Book House, visit our web site:
http://www.bakerbooks.com

To my wife Carolyn, who has been my proofreader and encourager throughout this whole process.

To my parents Tyrell and Oril Peart, whose sacrifice and support continue to bless the lives of their children.

To the memory of my first pastor, John Mlynar, who modeled the unprejudiced love that is to characterize Jesus' church.

CONTENTS

FOREWORD

I am pleased to have this opportunity to introduce you to this important new book from Norman Anthony Peart. It is a project that I believe has great significance for the church—and evangelical Christianity, in particular.

My decades of ministry in the fields of race relations and reconciliation have convinced me that the evangelical church in America still has much work to do in order to experience the unity that Jesus Christ desires. I have personally experienced the lack of understanding between black and white Christians and understand the divisions between other ethnic groups. However, I believe that the gospel calls us to come together to live out the Great Commandment (Matt. 22:37–40) and carry out the Great Commission (Matt. 28:19–20). And explaining how this can be accomplished is the strength of *Separate No More.*

Dr. Peart accurately shows that racial reconciliation has not been achieved because the church has viewed it as optional or peripheral to its primary mission. To engage this error, he identifies the historical problem, interprets the intended biblical pattern, and promotes the possibilities for change. This book will enrich pastors, local church leaders, leaders of Christian organizations, and lay Christians concerned about their role in racial reconciliation.

Key to this book is the presentation of an innovative model, the Reconciliation Continuum, to categorize churches' historic responses to racial reconciliation. Here, insight into personal and corporate failings may be gained and practical "how-to" steps are demonstrated for making reconciliation a reality.

The pursuit of racial reconciliation has played an important role in my life and ministry as evident in the two organizations the Lord has used me to establish: the John M. Perkins Foundation for Reconciliation and Development in Jackson, Mississippi, and the Christian Community Development Association in Chicago, Illinois. Thus, I am particularly pleased to commend Dr. Peart's volume to you, for it furthers my vision for reconciliation and equips the church of the twenty-first century to resolve this issue for the sake of Christ's church. I wholeheartedly encourage you to read and apply its message.

John M. Perkins

ACKNOWLEDGMENTS

I would like to thank a special group of people for their role in moving this book from a thought to a reality.

First, to the staff of Baker Book House:

Mary Suggs, thank you for your skill and insights as an editor that have forced me to think, rethink, and work to clarify the concepts of this book.

Bob Hosack, thank you for the opportunity to fulfill a desire the Lord has laid on my heart.

Jim Weaver, thank you for the insights that helped me understand and operate within "the system."

Second, my church at Grace Bible Fellowship:

Thank you, saints, for the opportunity to put into practice what I preach. It is truly a privilege to be your pastor.

Finally, and foremost, my wife and sons:

Thank you for keeping me focused on what really matters during the process of writing this book and for encouraging me every step of the way. I could not have accomplished this without your permission.

INTRODUCTION

As I stepped into the foyer after the service, I felt a little uncom-
fortable being at this church for the first time. I had been in
numerous churches before this. Having gone to Bible college and
now beginning seminary, I had had various opportunities to
visit different churches. But here I felt a little out of place. I
knew why. This was a white church and I was the only black
person there. Still, I was there at my roommate's invitation so
I decided to use the opportunity to get to know the people around
me. What other choice did I have? He was driving!

Finally a familiar face, a fellow seminarian appeared. As
we talked, he asked me at what church in the area I was a
member. I said I had not yet joined a church and that was the
reason I was visiting his church. It was easy to see his dis-
comfort and he quickly encouraged me to visit a predominantly
black church he was aware of on the other side of town.

As I think about this incident, and I have a few times
since it occurred, two interesting questions come to
mind. First, why was I, a black man, a little nervous in
church? Wasn't I there to worship like everyone else?
Second, why did this fellow seminarian not try to sell
me on his church and encourage me to join there? He

would probably have done that if the visitor to his church had been white. The answer to these questions is the same: That's the way it is. If the race of the individuals involved were switched, we would not be totally surprised if the responses were still the same. The history of race relations in the United States and in American evangelical Christianity explains the racial divide that exists among churches and Christians today. Yet the Bible is very clear that this is not God's intention for his church, so the question to ask is, How can this great divide be removed? *Separate No More* is written to address this question.

The book is for pastors and concerned Christians who seek a biblical basis for, and a better understanding of, their role in the ministry of racial reconciliation. The book's premise is that racial reconciliation has not been achieved in and between evangelical churches in America because this aspect of ministry is wrongly viewed as optional or peripheral to the purpose and central focus of the church.

Most Christians today would say that racism is wrong and would identify human sinfulness as the primary cause of it. Unfortunately, that is where most Christians stop, far short of evaluating their own attitudes and how racism affects them and those around them. But a failure to proceed beyond this point in our consideration of race hinders our ability to understand its impact on American Christianity. A closer examination shows that racism has used the American church to battle against God's will and purpose for his people. Racism has accomplished this goal by encouraging numerous rationalizations for the church's positions on slavery and racial discrimination, positions that are inconsistent with the message of the Bible. These rationalizations have included economic, political, social, biological, and even theological explanations for negative treatment of blacks. Because racism has so weakened the ministry of the church, racial reconciliation must today be at the heart of the American evangelical church's mission.

The book will examine three broad areas that have an impact on how churches deal with racial and ethnic differences: the historical problem, the intended biblical pattern, and the possibilities for change. To begin, we will look at the historical basis for the race problem. Just as we need to go back to the beginning of the Bible to understand sin's impact on social interactions, so we need to go back to the early history of this nation to understand the role of race in the present interactions of black and white Christians in America.

The first four chapters show the changing relationship between African American and white Christians. The first chapter examines the slavery period in which race relations are characterized by a separation between blacks and whites. In the early stages of this period the spiritual condition of blacks is overlooked because they were viewed as soul-less and therefore not redeemable. Over time this perspective evolved into a concern for the spiritual condition of blacks as some white Christians sought to see slaves come to a saving knowledge of Jesus Christ. Even then separate worship services were instituted. In the slavery period race relations can be characterized as *separate and unconcerned,* and later, *separate but concerned.*

The second chapter examines the postslavery period, which establishes new boundaries and standards for interaction between the races. Blacks and whites worked to establish separate churches and denominations to meet the needs of their own racial community, and although many whites of that period viewed the relationship between the races as "separate but equal," a more accurate characterization would be *separate and uninvolved.*

The third chapter presents the period of the Civil Rights movement in which the cry for black power and equal rights created a deeper tension in the relationship of blacks and whites. Many evangelical white churches viewed the focus of the Civil Rights movement as too worldly, even though it was founded in and supported by the Black Church, and for this reason opposed the movement and its goals. This period can be described as *separate and alarmed.*

The period of the post–Civil Rights movement to the present is the focus of chapter 4. Although this period boasts of more cooperation and interaction between black and white Christians and churches, there is still a great divide between the two groups. Blacks and whites are still separate on Sunday and largely without intimate interracial relationships throughout the week. Although black and white Christians may share an evangelical doctrine, they are separate in life. Therefore, the period can be described as *separate but evangelical.*

The final chapter of this part sums up the damage that is presently experienced because of the racism that has historically plagued our country.

The second part of the book, the intended biblical pattern, shows that the New Testament church viewed the ministry of racial or ethnic reconciliation as central and pivotal to the church's purpose. The prominence given to divisive ethnic issues and the remedies the church adopted are highlighted as patterns for the church's ministry in the world today.

The final section of the book gives practical suggestions for making the ministry of racial reconciliation an integral part of our lives. Insights from a diverse group of pastors on the implementation of multiracial ministry in a local church setting are invaluable. (See the appendix for brief biographical sketches of these pastors and their respective ministries.)

My own experience in multiracial ministry helps me provide an honest and straightforward look at the issues that are salient in the endeavor to achieve racial reconciliation. Having studied in predominantly white schools and having worked in both predominantly white and black churches, I have heard many of the important issues that are commonly raised by both of these groups. Practical suggestions are presented to assist readers to work through these issues and to develop their own strategy for being actively involved in the ministry of racial reconciliation.

There are two issues that I feel I must address before proceeding. First, although I know that our understanding of race is a concept that has been created by our unique history and does not have the same meaning in the Bible, it is a concept we must deal with because of its importance in our society. Because race is an aspect of how we view ourselves and also shapes our social interactions with others, we cannot trivialize the concept's significance and still minister effectively to the whole person. As sociologist W. I. Thomas said, "If men define situations as real, they are real in their consequences." For this reason, even though we may reject our society's understanding of race as unbiblical, we must not abandon the use of the concept. Having a proper understanding of race in our culture allows us to determine its effect on the lives of those around us.

Second, I want to highlight the important truth that biblical reconciliation is a working of the Holy Spirit and not the result of carefully crafted strategies or plans. This book contains insights and suggestions offered humbly with the prayer that they might be used for the addressing of this important problem in Christianity. The book is not offered as a cake recipe—"do this and succeed." Rather it is my desire that it will be used of the Lord to heighten the urgency and purposefulness of every Christian in yielding his or her life to the ministry of spiritual and racial reconciliation.

PART 1

THE HISTORICAL PROBLEM

To understand the racial divide that exists among evangelical churches and Christians today, we must go back in our history to see how the chasm first formed and then widened through the years. A significant historical foundation for the present racial division within evangelicalism exists, and race continues to play an important role in the contemporary witness of the church. It's true that through the years many white churches have assisted oppressed blacks in America, but the more common scenario has been the neglect of racial reconciliation by white Christians and churches. As a response to such neglect, many black churches are complacent when it comes to participation in reconciliation endeavors today. Though the church is called to transform society, the divide that exists among Christians simply mirrors the cultural and societal tensions in America, and in the area of racial reconciliation, the church has had little impact.

ONE

SEPARATE AND UNCONCERNED

The foundation of the structure of racism that has historically separated black and white Christians in the United States was laid in the early centuries of this country's existence. I will refer to this period of nearly two and one-half centuries as the slavery period. It begins a few decades after the first recorded landing of Africans in Virginia in 1619 and ends with the official abolition of slavery in 1865 with the passing of the Thirteenth Amendment. In this period the church, with few exceptions, shadowed the relationship between the races that was evident in the broader society. This pattern is apparent as the period is more closely examined.

The 1600s

In early Colonial society blacks were actually viewed as human beings and the church treated them as fellow humans in need of salvation. Therefore, twelve years after the founding of the first English colony in Jamestown, Virginia, when Africans were introduced into the early Colonies, their status was changed from slave to indentured servant because of their religious conversion. The Colonial government had purchased twenty Negroes, three of whom were women, from a Dutch frigate and had then distributed these individuals to private settlers. These Africans had been baptized, and according to English law, which governed Virginia, any slave who had converted to Christianity had to be freed. The theory behind this practice was that infidels could be enslaved as a means of communicating the gospel to them, but upon their conversion to Christianity, they had to be freed.[1] The fact that the same rules were applied to these blacks as to whites in the colonial community shows that the differentiation between the races was not as strong as it was to become in this century.

Just a few decades later there were clear evidences that blacks and whites in Colonial society and churches were viewed as separate and unequal on the basis of race. In 1630 a Virginia court sentenced Hugh Davis to "be soundly whipped before an assembly of Negroes and others, for abusing himself to the dishonor of God and shame of Christians, by defiling his body in lying with a Negroe; which fault he is to acknowledge next Sabbath day." In 1640 Robert Sweet was required "to do penance in church according to the laws of England, for getting a negroe woman with child and the woman [to be] whipt."[2] In 1691 another law in Virginia called for the banishing of any white man or woman who married a Negro, mulatto, or Indian.[3]

Virginia was the first colony to officially recognize slavery with an act passed in 1661 that made an indentured servant who ran away with a slave responsible for a master's loss during the slave's absence.[4] Other colonies struggled for a few more decades with the decision to adopt slavery, but time saw the objections give way and the institution was soon adopted.

Because the international slave trade had already firmly established a pattern of black enslavement and because there was no deep-seated opposition to the institution of slavery in the colonies, the increased life expectancy during the second half of the seventeenth century just made it a matter of time before slavery would replace indentured servitude as a major source of cheap labor.[5]

In the early Colonial period the most important antislavery movements were those of the Quakers (Society of Friends) and Puritans whose opposition to the institution was based strongly on religious principles. The Quakers were the pioneering antislavery church in America, yet it still needs to be noted that many, if not most, of the prosperous Friends in all colonies held slaves and participated in the slave trade up until the eve of the Revolutionary War. Also, whereas the dissenters to slavery in most of the other denominations published pamphlets and sermons condemning slavery, the Quakers did not.[6]

The first protest against slavery to be noted in the Colonies was uttered by Puritan Roger Williams. His plea for the captive Pequot Indians in 1637 was limited in its application but showed his belief that "perpetual slaverie" was an injustice.[7] Williams's perspective explains why the first positive legislation against Negro slavery was enacted in the colony that he founded, Rhode Island. By a Rhode Island statute in 1652, Negroes were to be held in service for only a limited number of years and were then to be set free in the same manner as English servants. Yet this law was only in effect in Providence and Warwick, and slavery was not long afterward found to be more profitable in Rhode Island than in other parts of New England.[8]

Although taking tremendous steps to distinguish themselves from the social pattern of the world, Puritans still manifested the extent to which they were influenced by this pattern. Puritans John Eliot and Cotton Mather were very concerned that Negroes were treated as animals and that little care was focused on their immortal souls. Eliot gave a lot of his personal time to instruct slaves and Mather published

Rules for the Society of Negroes, which urged kind treatment of slaves and encouraged their religious instruction. Unfortunately the influence of Eliot and Mather was limited because their main concern was with the moral and life conditions of the slaves and they did not take a stand supporting emancipation or the abolition of slavery.

With the adoption of Negro slaves as the primary workforce in America, the belief of whites that blacks were inferior was strongly reinforced and American slavery became exclusively identified with blacks, thereby becoming racial slavery. The way Negroes were viewed and treated was changing. Blacks were now viewed as "living tools," and treated as such, both in the South and in the North.[9]

The use of slaves mandated the adoption of new methods of disciplining the workforce. Masters could not motivate slaves to work through fear that they would lose their liberty—the approach that was used to motivate servants—so they had to create a different fear in slaves—fear that they would lose their lives. Actually masters did not want to kill their slaves and lose their investment, so they beat them as they did servants, but to get equal or greater work from slaves, they beat slaves more harshly than they did servants. Because death would relieve slaves of such abuse, and might therefore be longed for, the master had to be willing to somewhat restrain the beatings, stopping short of killing slaves but often maiming them to get them to comply. Inevitably some slaves were killed in the process. Realizing the possibility of this result, the Virginia Assembly in 1669 passed a law that legally protected masters who killed their slaves while disciplining them. Legislation to curb the growing problem of runaway slaves stated that it would "be lawful for any person or persons whatsoever, to kill and destroy such slaves by such ways and means as he, she, or they shall think fit, without accusation or impeachment of any crime for the same."[10] The law also stipulated that if a master killed a slave under these circumstances, he would be compensated with public funds.

The characterization of slaves as the property of whites, to be used for their personal benefit, is a key concept of the 1600s that dictated the relationship between blacks and whites and continued to influence that relationship into the next centuries.

The 1700s

The attitude that was generally held by the white clergy toward American slavery in the 1600s is largely uncertain because of the small number of historical documents from that period. But the early decades of the 1700s show clearly that many church leaders in the North and South viewed Negro slavery as compatible with the Christian faith. An example of a group that supported such a position on human bondage was the Colonial Anglicans.

The Anglican Church's mission group, the Society for the Propagation of the Gospel in Foreign Parts (S.P.G.), sent missionaries into all of the early American Colonies. From the start these missionaries attempted to evangelize Indians and Negro slaves, but their efforts displeased many masters. The masters expressed coolness toward the conversion of blacks because they feared that the conversion of slaves would obligate owners to view and treat these slaves as equals. They felt that the implications of such passages as Galatians 3:28, "there is neither slave nor free man, . . . for you are all one in Christ Jesus," would indirectly challenge the belief that was key to the institution of slavery—Negro inferiority.[11] To combat this reluctance, some missionaries urged the S.P.G. to send them suitable tracts or sermons that could be used to soften the resistance of the slave owners. The organization complied by printing relevant sermons that were preached by distinguished clergymen at the Society's anniversary gathering. One such address was given by William Fleetwood, bishop of Asaph, in 1711. Fleetwood emphasized that slaves were created by God with the same workmanship with which God created the planters and for that reason they needed to hear the gospel. At the same time he tried to relieve the fears of the slave owners by addressing their various concerns. One such concern was whether slaveholders could sell their slaves, having been taught that it is unlawful to sell Christians. Fleetwood asserted that since neither the teachings of Christ nor his kingdom prohibit individuals from selling what they possess, a slave who becomes a believer can still be sold because he or she continues to be a possession.[12]

The New England Puritans and the Quakers were clearly struggling within themselves to oppose slavery. The most significant evidence of antislavery sentiment in early Puritanism was the tract printed in 1701 by Chief-Judge Samuel Sewall, *The Selling of Joseph*. This three-page tract that was published in Boston and financed by Sewall himself focused primarily on the slave trade, but its arguments can be applied to slavery in general. In the tract Sewall focused on the natural and inalienable rights of all men to be free. This he argued is evident because, "these *Ethiopians* as black as they are; seeing they are the Sons and Daughters of the First *Adam,* the Brethren and Sisters of the Last Adam, and the Offspring of GOD; They ought to be treated with a Respect agreeable."[13]

Sewall's views were based on religious convictions and what he observed around him. He fought to have Negroes classified above horses and hogs and he even paid his Negro servant, Scipio, wages. Incredibly, however, Sewall did feel that there was too much of a difference in the color, conditions, and hair of blacks for them to ever live with whites.[14] It is not until a generation or two later that a Puritan antislavery writer, Nathaniel Appleton—a pastor's son whose tract *Considerations of Slavery* was published in 1767—takes an absolutely uncompromising stand for slavery's abolition.[15] As a whole, though, slavery continued to exist in New England along with the Puritans. In 1708 there were four hundred slaves in Boston.[16]

Although the Society of Friends had taken a strong stand opposing slavery in the 1600s, they struggled to maintain that unified stand in the 1700s. William Penn came into contact with slaves in Pennsylvania during his second American visit in 1699 and urged Friends to watch over the souls of their Negroes. He even attempted to persuade the Quaker-dominated legislature to legalize Negro marriages, but his attempt failed. Unfortunately the influence of slavery was so strong in the Quaker community that William Penn, founder of the "holy experiment" on the Delaware, was still a slave owner at his death in 1718. Still, the group's long-term efforts shine bright as is evidenced in the actions of such strong Quaker antislavery advocates as Anthony Benezet and John Woolman and a group of Philadelphia Quakers who organized the country's first antislavery society in 1775.

Whitefield and Wesley

The evangelical upsurge of the 1740s, generally known as the Great Awakening, impacted the Colonies from Massachusetts to Georgia. This movement received a greater response from Negroes than had Puritanism, Quakerism, Catholicism, or Anglicanism. One of the most influential evangelicals of this period, and one of the most interesting cases of evangelical compromise on the issue of slavery, was George Whitefield. Early in his career Whitefield had written the pamphlet *A Letter to the Inhabitants of Maryland, Virginia, North and South Carolina* in which he attacked inhabitants of these provinces because they treated their slaves worse than their own dogs. The date of the pamphlet's composition was January 1740, which was four months before he met the well-known Quaker abolitionist Anthony Benezet. Thus the sentiment expressed in Whitefield's tract should have been his own and not a pressured statement caused by his meeting with the noted abolitionist. In his pamphlet Whitefield took no definite stand against slavery as an unchristian institution, but his words implied a strong opposition to slavery. In speaking to slaveholders he stated, "I think God has a quarrel with you" and, "Whether it be lawful for Christians to buy slaves, and thereby encourage the nations from whence they are bought to be at perpetual war with each other, I shall not take upon me to determine; but sure I am it is sinful, when bought, to use them as bad as, nay worse than brutes."[17]

Whitefield's stated position in his pamphlet and his relationship with the Georgia colony, which was founded with its trustees forbidding the ownership of slaves, would have made those who knew Whitefield think that he was against slavery. But a year after writing the pamphlet, Whitefield was using all his influence to persuade the trustees of Georgia to legalize slavery in the colony. The reason for this change was Whitefield's belief that his Bethesda orphanage in Georgia could not be run without slave labor. In 1741 Whitefield wrote that it would be impossible to cultivate the land with just hired servants and the larger boys of the orphanage without "a few Negroes." In 1748 he wrote to the trustees of Georgia about his observation of life and labor on the Bethesda plantation: "This confirms me in the opinion I have entertained for a long time, that Georgia never can or will be a flourishing province without negroes are allowed."[18] Before slaves were allowed in the colony, Whitefield had purchased and was pleased to use them to support his orphanage. As early as 1747 Bethesda was benefiting from the profit Whitefield obtained from a slave-worked South Carolina plantation he called *Providence.*[19] In writing about the opportunity to have slaves in Georgia in a letter dated March 22, 1751, Whitefield rationalizes the institution of slavery for numerous reasons.

One writer states that Whitefield was one of the two most influential men in removing the prohibition against slavery in Georgia. When he died, Whitefield willed his Negroes, along with his buildings, lands, furniture, and books to the Countess of Huntingdon.[20] Similarly, many evangelicals of this period saw the great need for the slave's emancipation from sin and Satan's spiritual bondage, but could not see a need for their emancipation from slavery's physical bondage. The greatest tragedy, though, is that they did not see slavery as also a result of sin and Satan's spiritual bondage.

This devaluing of sin is evident in the early history of Methodism in America. Although John Wesley had written the tract *Thoughts upon Slavery* in 1774 strongly attacking slavery, the young movement he began chose not to take a strong stand against slavery. At the historic Christmas Conference of 1784, when the Methodist Episcopal Church was organized, a motion to condemn slavery as incompatible with Methodism was tabled. This decision to put the motion on hold was in response to fierce opposition that arose in the meeting. Methodist Bishop Thomas Coke later gave the reason as "our work being too infantile a state to push things to extremity."[21] The Reverend James O'Kelly, a native of Ireland, stood in strong opposition to the position of most of his fellow Methodists who favored black servitude. O'Kelly's position was in line with Wesley's as he stated, "Be well assured that slavery is a work of the flesh, assisted by the devil; a mystery of iniquity, that works like witchcraft, to darken your understanding, and harden your hearts against conviction."[22]

Impact of the American Revolution

When the Colonies entered into a war for their independence from England, the endeavor was heralded with cries for human freedom for all. But when these Colonies emerged from the struggle, in which five thousand blacks had fought, the rewards of victory were not extended to blacks. To make matters worse, the newly drafted Constitution declared that a slave was three-fifths of a man, or that it would take five slaves to equal three white men. John Hope Franklin notes that this inconsistency in America's founding fathers' view of human freedom has continued to affect American society.

> We are concerned here not so much for the harm that the founding fathers did to the cause they claimed to serve as for the harm that their moral legacy has done to every generation of their progeny. Having created a tragically flawed revolutionary doctrine and a constitution that did *not* bestow the blessings of liberty on its posterity, the founding fathers set the stage for every succeeding generation of Americans to apologize, compromise, and temporize on those principles of liberty that were supposed to be the very foundation of our system of government and way of life.[23]

In the North there was still a racial divide that was very evident at the end of this century. An example of this racial divide is the event that led to the formation of one of the oldest and most influential black denominations. In 1787 in Philadelphia, free Negroes Richard Allen and Absalom Jones and other black worshipers were pulled from their knees while praying and were forced to leave the whites-only section in the gallery of St. George Methodist Episcopal Church. The group had mistakenly knelt there to pray. Because of this incident the group left the white denomination and organized the Free African Society to offer mutual aid to Negro families in their time of need. The society was the parent body of the African Methodist Episcopal (A.M.E.) Church, which was established in 1816. Allen became the denomination's first bishop.[24]

Both the spiritual and the social environments of America in the 1700s were willing to embrace great compromise between what was held to be right and what was held to be convenient. Unfortunately what was held to be convenient consistently triumphed and set the stage for the great social and spiritual divisions of the 1800s.

1800–1865

There were four events in the early 1800s that caused the value of slaves, and America's commitment to slavery, to increase:

1. The legal prohibition of the importation of slaves from Africa into America after January 1, 1808
2. The country's expansion into the new lands of the Southwest
3. The growth of cotton production in the South
4. The decreased availability of cheap European labor

Because of the drastic increase in America's dependence on slaves, it became very important for slaves to produce offspring as a means of maintaining and perhaps even increasing the slave population. A benefit of America's dependence on slaves was the improvement of the slave's living conditions and physical treatment. These changes were made to improve the slave's chances for successful childbirth and the growth of children to maturity. Within the first three decades of the 1800s more than one million blacks were added to the South's population. During this time neither churches nor antislavery groups were able to slow the growth of slavery.[25] Also, because large numbers of slaves were so crucial to the maintenance of America's way of life, Colonial laws that had given masters and other whites great freedom in killing slaves were limited or discontinued in the 1800s. In 1821 South Carolina became the last of the slave states to declare that it was going to protect the lives of slaves. These laws had clearly moved slaves from a position of chattel to one more akin to human beings in the eyes of the state.

The Growth of Christianity among Slaves

During the 1600s and most of the 1700s, whites had had very little concern for the salvation of slaves and did little to introduce them to Christ. A primary reason for this lack of concern was the great separation between these two groups in society, a separation that hindered most whites from seeing slaves as people and having a need for salvation. In the 1800s evangelical churches began to focus intently on the spiritual condition of slaves, even though they continued to overlook the social wrongs of slavery. For this reason, by the eve of the Civil War, Christianity was strong in the slave community. The white community developed two means of meeting the worship needs of Christian slaves. The first was to allow them to worship with whites in the same church, though segregating them to the galleries or to back pews. The second, which occurred around the 1820s, was to allow some blacks to have their own services under the supervision of white clergymen. The slaves' exposure to formal Christian teaching, though, primarily depended on the will of their masters. Masters who allowed their slaves to receive such teachings did so for one of two reasons: the master's piety or the master's desire to use Christianity to his own advantage.

The religious piety or devotion of many masters, which seemed to show more evidence during this century,[26] motivated them to try to develop religious disciplines in their slaves by encouraging them to attend the master's church. Some slaves, though, would not attend because of their master's actions during the week. One example is the insight of Moses Roper, who said that when the master's slaves learned that he was a Baptist, they, "thinking him a very bad sample of what a professing Christian ought to be, would not join the connexion he belonged to, thinking they must be a very bad set of people."[27]

The desire to use the teachings of Christianity to prevent revolt and increase production led many masters to provide preachers to instruct their slaves. William Wells Brown, a former slave, believed that some planters—he cites those in Missouri—preferred a religious slave because the slave was taught "that God made him for a slave; and that, when whipped, he must not find fault,—for the Bible says, 'He that knoweth his master's will, and doeth it not shall be beaten with many stripes!'"[28] Even some slave owners began to preach to be sure of the message being proclaimed to their slaves. But their notable inconsistencies and hypocrisies hindered their credibility with the slaves.

In either case these masters would not allow their slaves to learn any doctrines of Christianity, such as the brotherhood of all believers, that would possibly result in their rebellion.[29] To keep slaves from receiving such teachings, masters would not allow white preachers to teach through the entire Bible in the presence of the slaves. Those who did not heed the warning were punished. Therefore, slaves grew to distrust white preachers because they were aware of the tremendous influence the slave masters had over them. What is amazing is that the power of the gospel was evident to these slaves, who were being oppressed by a perversion of the very same gospel. This is very evident in the narratives of many former slaves who noted the discrepancy between Scripture and what they were taught.

> There was one very kind hearted Episcopal minister whom I often used to hear; he was very popular with the colored people. But after he had preached a sermon to us in which he argued from the Bible that it was the will of heaven from all eternity we should be slaves, and our masters be our owners, most of us left him; for like some of the faint hearted disciples in early times we said,—"This is a hard saying, who can bear it?"[30]

On the other hand, there were many masters who opposed their slaves' attending worship services, and would use various means to hinder them from doing so. Some, however, were forced to give in when even floggings proved unsuccessful. The dignity and worth of the individual that are basic to the teachings of Christianity equipped slaves to defy ungodly authority while at the same time submitting to the Savior whom these slaves had come to love.

As a result of greater religious freedom being given to slaves, the number of black churches began to increase. This increase in the number of individual churches also led to the inception of various black denominations in the South, one of the most significant being Baptist. Black Baptists originated in the South and the first independent black Baptist congregations were organized during the last half of the 1700s. The black Baptists in the South sought to relate the teachings of Christianity to the lives of slaves on the southern plantations. Northern free blacks in the slavery period formed abolitionist missionary associations and societies, and their leaders organized the first regional black Baptist conventions. In 1831, however, the insurrection of black preacher Nat Turner caused much of the independence experienced by southern black Baptist churches to be curtailed. Black preachers were then limited in their rhetoric and black churches were brought under the supervision of white churches.

Antislavery Movements

The general improvement in the way slaves were treated in this century seemed sufficient enough reform to keep many white Christians from strongly advocating emancipation.[31] During this period the great work of the Quakers stood bright. Overall, by the dawn of the nineteenth century, Quakerism had cut its ties with Negro bondage. "This achievement is all the more significant because the Friends in numerous instances not only set their bondsmen free but assisted them financially, educationally, and otherwise to establish themselves as freemen."[32] Unfortunately, even though the Friends purged themselves of Negro bondage, they still showed signs of discrimination. Negroes were often denied Quaker membership, had to sit in special areas during worship, and were denied burial with other Quakers.[33]

The antislavery movement was also active outside the Quaker community, although the Quakers were the most focused and achieved the greatest results. Denominations such as the Methodists and Baptists over time began to combine their efforts to advocate universal liberty. Theologians, humanitarians, and politicians also combined their efforts to advocate a prohibition of the slave trade in the northern states, and later a national prohibition of the slave trade. This was achieved in 1807 and, appeasing the conscience of many whites for a time and lulling them into thinking that this was a deathblow to slavery, was followed by a pause in the development of the antislavery movement.

A significant abolitionist sentiment arose in the 1830s, with the single most powerful agent being the American Anti-Slavery Society, which was launched in Philadelphia on December 4, 1833. William Lloyd Garrison, an early organizer of the American Anti-Slavery Society, drafted a *Declaration of Sentiments* in 1831 that was clearly based on democratic and religious convictions. The document called slavery a sinful and criminal institution that should move the nation to abolish slavery, repent, and free all slaves. Slaves were not to be colonized somewhere else, but black Americans were to be given all the privileges and opportunities of white Americans. This was fervently called for, "With entire confidence in the overruling justice of God, we plant ourselves upon the Declaration of our Independence and the truths of divine revelation as upon the Everlasting Rock."[34]

But Garrison's declaration was not the writing of the abolitionist movement that had the greatest impact. In 1852 Harriet Beecher Stowe (the daughter, wife, and sister of ministers) published *Uncle Tom's Cabin*. The message of this abolitionist novel reverberated throughout the country. The book sold ten thousand copies the first week and three hundred thousand copies the first year.

A prominent evangelical of this time was the evangelist Charles Grandison Finney. His "moral theology" provided a theological framework and moral impulse on which some evangelical abolitionists stood to argue their position. Although Finney personally held an antislavery position and strongly referred to slavery as a sin, he was unwilling to publicly advocate the cause of abolition because he feared that such a stand would diminish the pursuit of his primary task— saving souls.[35]

Finney also made a clear distinction between the abolition of slavery and amalgamation. The former he favored but the latter he feared, primarily because of the effect it could have on unity within local churches. Finney came to realize this in his own church, the Chatham Street Chapel in New York, when members became disgruntled because black and white choirs sat separately in the front of the church. For this reason he favored the segregation of blacks and whites within the Chatham Street Chapel.[36]

Although the Anti-Slavery Society was not violent, nor did they advocate the violent overthrow of the slave institution, a strong southern campaign was waged against them. Southern political and religious groups worked hard to have the people of the North curb the activities of the society. For instance, the South Carolina legislature adopted a committee report on December 16, 1836, charging that abolitionism was "treason against the Union." They requested that northern governments make it a criminal offense to write, publish, and distribute any newspaper or tracts that could incite slave insurrections. Within the next three months, six other states passed similar measures. Unfortunately this southern protest drew sympathetic response from the North. Many northern cities from Boston to Philadelphia passed resolutions denouncing abolitionists. Also the fact that abolitionists based their fervent opposition to slavery on democratic and religious convictions drew southern ministers into the controversy. This occurred in spite of the insistence of these ministers for decades that slavery was not an issue for the church but for the state alone. The early debate between northern and southern ministers over slavery became so bitter that three of the largest Protestant denominations split apart by midcentury primarily because of this issue.

Denominational Splits

As abolitionists in the denominations pushed for a strong stand against slavery, denominational splits were inevitable for two reasons. First, many of the churches during this century had a strong desire to focus on the spiritual needs of the slaves while ignoring their social rights.[37] Second, and the most significant reason, in many cases the clergy and churches could not strongly oppose slavery because they were deeply intertwined in the institution of slavery. Many ministers were dependent on wealthy planters for their financial support and for this reason many taught the divine origin of slavery, thereby encouraging its continuation. This is evident in older slave states like Virginia and South Carolina where churches owned slaves and hired them out for the support of the minister. An advertisement to such an end was found in the *Charleston Courier,* of February 12, 1835.

FIELD NEGROES, By Thomas Gadsden.

On Tuesday, the 17th Instant, will be sold, at the north of the Exchange, at ten o'clock, a prime gang of ten NEGROES, accustomed to the culture of cotton and provisions, belonging to the INDEPENDENT CHURCH, in *Christ's Church Parish.* * * * Feb. 6.[38]

The intermingling of the church and slavery can also be seen in the observation of the Reverend Philo Tower who traveled through the South for three years. He noted that what was more lamentable than the physical cruelty of slavery, as great as it was, was the impact slavery had on the church in the South.

> But what is the amount of *religious instruction* enjoyed by the slaves? inquire, many of my northern friends. To which I answer; first, that no less than 665,563 slaves are owned by southern *divines* and their churches. Only think of that, dear reader, six hundred and sixty five thousand five hundred and sixty-three human, redeemed, immortal beings, are owned soul and body, by these *successors* of great PAUL and PETER, to be worked, bought, sold, flogged, rented and imprisoned, &c., &c. At one thousand dollars per head, which may be a fair average price for this clerical stock; then these *followers,* nay, *religious teachers* of Him who had not where to lay his head, are worth the round sum of six hundred and sixty-five million, five hundred and sixty-three thousand dollars, invested in human beings. Could ancient Roman or Grecian Pagan priests boast so much? No never. . . . Of what avail are the prayers, sermons, public teachings and lofty pretensions to piety, of a man who can sell his brother into perpetual bondage?[39]

The Reverend Albert Barnes noted that it is wrong to say that the Church of Jesus Christ is the "bulwark of slavery" in light of the fact that it was a major cause in the abolition of slavery in the Roman empire and in England. But he laments the fact that the church in America was unable to "detach" itself from slavery and to totally stand against it and therefore was unable to cause slavery's demise. The greatest fault of the church in America, according to Barnes, was that it had not influenced its society, a large portion of which was connected to the church.

> The church will affect the institution of slavery, or the institution of slavery will affect the church. It will send out a healthful moral influence to secure its removal, or the system will send out a corrupt influence into the church itself,

to mould the opinions of its members, to corrupt their piety, to make them apologists for oppression and wrong, and to secure its sanction in sustaining the system itself.[40]

The three major evangelical denominations in which these splits occurred were the Presbyterians, the Methodists, and the Baptists. Let us examine briefly each of these splits to show the prominent role slavery played in dividing these well-established denominations.

Presbyterians

The first denominational split took place in 1837 when the Presbyterian Church, one of the largest Protestant denominations in the United States, broke apart. Although the general assembly of the Presbyterian Church denounced slavery in 1818 "as utterly inconsistent with the law of God" and "as totally irreconcilable with the spirit and principles of the gospel of Christ," a call a few decades later for Presbyterians to not participate in slavery resulted in the denomination's division.[41]

The steps toward this division began in 1836 when a committee was established to consider and to report to that year's assembly whether the general assembly should adopt a strong abolitionist position. Conservative Presbyterians in the North and the South, who were in favor of slavery, began to threaten that if the abolitionists pressed for the denomination to take a strong stand against slavery, they would withdraw from the general assembly. A major support for this proslavery position came on the eve of the assembly by the esteemed and powerful Charles Hodge of Princeton Theological Seminary. Hodge published a strong article warning that if the abolitionist position were adopted, a division in the church would quickly result. In the article Hodge strongly argued that abolitionists' teaching was erroneous and had a harmful impact on the nation and the church. He believed that slavery was scripturally acceptable and, therefore, not morally outlawed.

Hodge even argued that the great duty of the South was not emancipation, since Jesus never addressed this subject, but the improvement of the life conditions of the slaves.[42]

There were many northerners who disagreed with the abolitionists. These individuals argued that slavery was a civil issue in which the church had no right to interfere. The proslavery arguments were effective, for when the assembly gathered in May of 1836 the members of the committee, with one exception, had prepared a report in agreement with the South's position. The meeting of 1836 ended in a nondecision and the motion on slavery was tabled. The slavery issue and other doctrinal issues, relating to original sin and revivalistic activities, made a denominational split inevitable. Instead of acknowledging that slavery was a sinful system, many Presbyterians in the southern region gathered in 1858 and finalized their departure by organizing the United Synod of the Presbyterian Church in the U.S.A.

Methodists

The Methodists expressed their disapproval of slavery in 1784 when the denomination was formally organized in America. The failure to enforce national rules against slavery allowed for individual decisions by local parishes to adopt the slave system, especially those in the South. Still, the Methodists were very committed to the evangelization of slaves. By 1817 the denomination had a black membership of forty-three thousand and blacks made up 40 percent of the Methodists in Carolina and Georgia. The long-term aim of the Methodist leaders was to recolonize these Negro believers in Africa, and Liberia seemed an ideal relocation site.

As the general body of Methodism struggled over the issue of slavery, abolitionists in the North began forcing the issue. Their first step came in 1843 when a large defection of antislavery Methodists organized the Wesleyan Methodist Church. The next year the general conference decided that a southern bishop, James O. Andrew, could no longer hold office because he owned slaves. In reaction to this decision the southern Methodists withdrew from the denomination and in May 1845 established the Methodist Episcopal Church, South, a proslavery denomination with about five hundred thousand members.

Baptists

The Baptists played a major role in the liberation of slaves for religious reasons. The number of freedmen was said to have increased by 150 percent from 1800 to 1810, in comparison to previous decades, because of the Baptists.[43] The Baptists in the nation, who were loosely organized around societies and boards for missionary purposes, divided in 1845, a year after the Methodist schism. In 1845 the struggle between the northern and southern Baptists came to a head when the Alabama Baptists asked the Home Mission Society to appoint a slaveholder for missionary service. After much labor to find a way around the issue, the board decided to not appoint as a missionary any individual who owned, and wanted to continue owning, slaves.[44] On May 8, 1845, southern Baptist leaders gathered in Augusta, Georgia, and speedily organized the Southern Baptist Convention. This new convention was more tightly organized than anything the loosely associated Baptists in America had experienced to that point. They supported slavery and held the belief that the Negro was inferior and cursed, being a descendant of Ham.

The Southern Clergy

Overall, southern religion played several important roles in making secession of southern states possible. The most significant of those roles was that of a mentor. When the Presbyterian, Methodist, and Baptist denominations divided more than fifteen years before the South's secession and the Civil War, "a strong national cohesiveness was broken and an example was set for future political division."[45] Southern religion also fulfilled its mentor role through its leadership in the great national war when southern clergymen stood in the forefront of the struggle for southern independence. They cared for parishes, served as chaplains, and even enlisted in great numbers in the fighting ranks. In many cases a clergyman would organize a fighting company and then become its captain.

Clearly the southern evangelical clergy, which comprised a majority of religious leaders in the South, moved in step with southern society. They had opposed slavery during the 1700s, but as slavery became more entrenched in southern society, they first adopted a position of silence on the issue in the early 1800s and of militant defense of it in the latter 1800s. This militant position was verbalized in the argument that slavery was a civil matter and not a religious concern. As such, the laws of the South, which had already legitimized slavery, had given a final word to which the church had to comply. This stance was most likely introduced by Presbyterians in the South and was later adopted and implemented by most southern denominations.

This strong defense of slavery resulted in four themes that became primary to the preaching of the southern pulpit.

1. The foundation on which all other themes were based was that slavery was a God-ordained and biblically sanctioned institution.
2. Those who opposed slavery were anti-God and anti-Bible. Therefore, the North and especially abolitionists were attacked as infidels.
3. The doctrine of the inferiority of the black race was accepted. Because of this doctrine, teachings on the rights and equality of mankind were generally absent from the southern pulpit.

4. Evangelicals needed to give religious instruction to slaves, which would lead to their conversion and greater acceptance of their position in life.[46]

The fact that slavery had become embedded in the economy, culture, mentality, and even the religion of the South made a division with the North inevitable. For this reason it took a conflict far more horrible than the Revolutionary War before the constitutional statement "all men are created equal" would be applied to all men.

SEPARATE AND UNINVOLVED

If the slavery period is the foundation of the structure of racism in this country, then the period spanning the end of slavery to the beginning of the modern Civil Rights movement is its first floor. This period extends from the late 1860s to the mid-1950s. With the abolishing of slavery, this period becomes a national opportunity for racial reconciliation. Tragically, society's choice is segregation and this choice is adopted by the evangelical church, which divides along racial lines.

After the Civil War

With the end of slavery in the South, monumental changes challenged a society that had grown accustomed to the order slavery had imposed on life. For southern blacks the initial period of rejoicing and thanksgiving on hearing of their emancipation was quickly followed by an overwhelming burden of responsibility. Such a feeling is understandable for those who had spent all of their lives being forced to live as children, especially for those who were now in their seventies and eighties.[1] But the Reconstruction period allowed some blacks the opportunity to serve with distinction in prominent political positions.

Southern whites faced different issues. They had lost decisively on the battlefield, had lost two billion dollars in slaves as property, and their society was now being controlled by northern whites who allowed blacks full political and civil rights. For southern whites there was the great question of how they would regain control of their own destiny and there was the great fear that they would be ruled by the very people they once called slaves. The poverty of the postwar South made many whites feel dependent and humiliated, which they had always viewed as suitable characteristics of blacks rather than whites. For Christians and all people of both racial groups, decisions made during this period of Reconstruction, from 1865 to 1877, would shape race relations for decades to come.

During Reconstruction the relationship of the southern states to the federal government was reestablished, with the federal government gradually giving the southern states great independence to reconstruct their society. This power was then used, during this period, and more so in the post-Reconstruction period, to legally, economically, and socially segregate,[2] or isolate, blacks. The South's legal policy was legitimized by the Supreme Court's 1896 decision, *Plessy v. Ferguson,* which supported the South's "separate but equal" policy.[3] The *separate* was strictly adhered to, but the *equal* was rarely achieved. Racial segregation laws, known as Jim Crow laws, became an important means of preserving and legitimizing the established order of white supremacy and black subordination. Once segregation was made legal, any opposition to it was classified as illegal activity, thereby removing the legal rights of blacks. When whites considered that their attempts to keep blacks in their place through legal segregation failed, other means of attaining the same goal, such as through the Ku Klux Klan[4] and lynching,[5] became legal in the South.

The Church during This Period

In this social setting the most characteristic view of black Christians that was held by southern white evangelicals was that their practice of Christianity was inferior to that of whites. Many white evangelicals believed that, although blacks had received proper doctrinal training while under slavery, after emancipation they easily strayed from this civil and accurate form of Christianity. For this reason, many southern clergy argued that blacks needed to continue worshiping with whites, although separated in the worship service, and many took steps to keep blacks under their supervision.

Many southern evangelical pastors and churches provided for another need of black evangelicals, which was the education of their pastors. This assistance sometimes resulted in a warm interracial relationship after blacks had separated from white churches. Unfortunately, however, most white evangelical churches did not assist black churches and denominations. A major reason for this lack of support was the great pressure that was placed on most white clergymen to not stray from accepted racial views and practices. Assistance resulting in black improvement would have been considered a threat to the South's social order. As one writer noted, "racial heresy was more dangerous to a preacher's reputation than theological speculation."[6] Most clergy who worked to make the racial system less harsh still preached black inferiority and white superiority because they were expected to do so.

Seeking to have their needs met, many southern black churches aligned themselves with northern white denominations that were more than willing to assist them. These northern denominations provided valuable financial support for building construction, education of clergy, and the establishment of black colleges in the South. Unfortunately over time black churches realized that many of these northern white churches and denominations were only a little less paternalistic and racist than their southern counterparts. In response to the northern assistance to blacks, some southern clergy instigated the burning of black schools and churches by arguing that these buildings represented a threat to southern order in that they were built with money from northern denominations.

But blacks clearly held the final word on how and where they would worship after emancipation. For blacks in the South, emancipation gave them the opportunity to focus on themselves as a race, especially as the policy of segregation removed them from an active participation in the broader society. During the Civil War, many black northern evangelists went South to convert blacks, and many of these converts felt that joining a black church was essential for them to experience the fullness of their emancipation. Blacks left white denominations in great numbers, with the loss of blacks from some denominations amounting to 90 percent of their total membership. By 1870 most southern blacks had left white evangelical churches that practiced the type of segregated worship that was typical during slavery. Many of these individuals joined churches that had been begun by either northern blacks or biracial denominations.[7] Their withdrawal from white denominations led to a growth period for black evangelicalism in the South.

The Black Church

The discrimination expressed by southern white Christians and the condescending sympathy of northern white Christians fostered the development of an independent black church movement. One of the most significant of these new church movements was the merging of various black Baptist conventions to form the National Baptist Convention, U.S.A., in 1895. This was a significant step as it occurred in a period, 1890–1910, of many attempts to suppress black freedom. Between 1890 and 1906 the number of black Baptist ministers increased from 5,500 to over 17,000. The National Baptist Convention, U.S.A., was an influential organization in the life of African Americans and worked diligently for their social and religious improvement. The National Baptist Convention, U.S.A., Inc., continues to be the largest of all the black denominations and is considered the largest African American organization in existence.

Although black Baptists founded the earliest churches and still have the largest membership, the Methodist movement among African Americans organized the first black denominations. Richard Allen was one of the first to do this (see chapter 1). These denominations were the first national organizations for blacks in America. Free blacks formed black Methodist churches, conferences, and denominations in the North.[8]

Clearly the first incentive for black spiritual and ecclesiastical independence was not based on religious doctrine or polity, but it was a response to the offensive acts of racial segregation and the stark inconsistencies between what was taught and practiced that blacks experienced in white churches. The rebellion of black Christians resulted in "the Black Church." The Black Church became, therefore, a symbol for and means of black independence and rebellion.

At this point in our history, there was a major distinction in the focus of black and white evangelical Christians. White evangelical Christians had developed a strong separation in their theological worldview between personal salvation and social influence. A priority was given to leading individuals to saving faith without challenging those individuals to allow their new spiritual relationship to influence society. For black evangelical Christians there could be no separation between faith and practice because of the great needs that were evident in their communities. The reality of a personal relationship with Jesus had to be evident in the social actions of the faith community.

One major effect of the movement of blacks out of white churches was that it removed the contact of blacks and whites in a sacred setting. This is important because the church was a key place where individuals came into contact and where deeper relationships could be fostered.[9] This was especially the case in the rural areas of the South. As white churches became predominantly white, black culture began to seem more alien and was feared even more than it was during the slavery years. For white evangelicals the world was viewed as sinful and threatening, and blacks were seen as a major reason for that threat. Blacks could not see much difference in the whites they knew under slavery and the whites they now knew in freedom. The separation of evangelical black Christians from their white brethren limited their ability to encounter white evangelicals who embodied the realities of true Christianity. Therefore, black evangelicals were left to see the world and especially the whites who controlled it as sinful and a threat to their very existence.

Relationships in the North

In the North the interaction between the races during this period appeared calmer than in the South. A major reason was that illegal violence, overlooked by those in authority, was used by northern whites to keep political and economic control. This racial oppression was not usually reported, so it was not obvious to northern whites and to some blacks, and the accounts that did get out were considered unique occurrences. Another reason for the apparent calm was the comparatively small number of blacks who lived in the North. For this reason, in the decades of the 1870s through the 1890s the small number of northern Negroes was not perceived as an economic threat to European immigrants, such as the Germans and Irish, and they were therefore able to live a somewhat integrated existence. In most large urban areas, such as New York, whites had little contact with blacks and knew very little about their daily lives. There were, however, some white churches in northern cities that would allow, and even welcome, small numbers of blacks to attend.

Scientific Theories

Despite the relatively peaceful coexistence, there were clear evidences that northerners had views of blacks that were similar to those of southerners. One such evidence of this was the widespread acceptance of scientific theories developed in the late 1800s and the early 1900s that purported to prove black inferiority. Charles Darwin's use of the subtitle "The Preservation of Favored Races in the Struggle for Life" to refer to animals in his *Origin of the Species* in 1859 inspired some to apply his theories to humans. Throughout the 1800s and the early 1900s, scientists in England and the United States attempted to prove that blacks were intellectually inferior to whites in accordance with Darwin's theory. In the 1800s scientists measured skulls to show that the brains of blacks weighed less than the brains of whites. In the 1900s scientists focused on genetics.[10] Protestant clergyman Josiah Strong wrote a book in 1885 asserting that the "Anglo Saxon race" was destined to inhabit every part of the earth. This result would be the "survival of the fittest" as Anglo Saxons would supplant the weaker and native races of those conquered areas. Strong identified Anglo Saxons with what it meant to be a Christian and, therefore, identified whites as God's ideal for Christianity.[11]

Turn of the Century

The relationship of black and white Christians in the twentieth century would not greatly improve. The focus of both groups was inward. One very important result of the discrimination of southern white Christians and the condescending sympathy of northern white Christians was that the Black Church used all of its strengths and resources for meeting the needs of the black community, becoming its very center. Black churches educated, fed, informed, empowered, honored, and organized the black community. Even the black secular institutions that were established beginning in the 1900s, such as the National Association for the Advancement of Colored People in 1909 and the National Urban League in 1911, were often founded with the help and support of Black Church leaders. This was so much the case that the membership of many of these organizations often overlapped with Black Church membership. In some cases Black Church members worked to start these organizations to create an outlet that could be used to further their influence in the black community without affecting the focus and working of their churches. Also some of the nation's best black colleges, such as Morehouse and Spelman, were founded at this time in the basement of black churches. Morehouse was organized to train ministers and Spelman focused on training missionaries and teachers.

The Migration North

Beginning in 1910 the harsh effects of southern segregation and the opportunities created by the industrial revolution in the North caused many blacks to move north. Whereas the population pattern of Negroes prior to the 1900s was primarily southern and rural, with 90 percent of Negroes living below the Mason-Dixon line, after this period the Negro population became more northern and urban. As blacks now in the North competed with whites for everything from employment opportunities to recreational facilities, tension between the two groups escalated. Racial relations became a major national issue and not just a southern problem.

The North was now primed for racial conflict, especially since most northerners had abandoned working for the rights of blacks in the South by the late 1800s, having accepted their condition. To be more exact, most northerners had come to agree with southern prejudices. Throughout the period from the Civil War to the 1920s, northern newspapers, magazines, and plays justified segregation, lynching, and black subordination in the South. Many northern journalists and playwrights viewed blacks as stupid, morally deficient, criminal in nature, and inferior to whites. The migration of blacks to the North was identified as the cause of riots, an increase in sinful behavior, and urban deterioration.

The Attitude of the Church

A similarly negative view of blacks was also evident among Christians. The crudest form of this attack from a biblical perspective was Charles Carroll's *The Negro a Beast.* The book, which included derogatory pictures, argued that there was no biblical evidence that blacks were the sons of Ham or even human beings. Instead the author argued that blacks were beasts who were without souls.

Since the end of Reconstruction, changes had occurred in respect to the position of Negroes in society, but most white Protestant church leaders generally had little interest in relating the social message of Christianity to the daily problems and social issues confronting Negroes. Many of these leaders argued that Christianity did not have a social message regarding the condition of Negroes and that their only responsibility was to communicate the gospel to them. There were some white leaders, however, who believed that their responsibility included addressing the social issues Negroes faced.

As in the period of slavery, these differing views on race relations were more a regional characteristic than a denominational one. Many holding to the same doctrinal positions in the same denominations would have dissimilar views on race relations based on where they lived. In the South the answer to race relations was evangelism under southern white guidance. Possibly the major reason that southern denominations had little if no interest in the social implications of the race problem is that they generally accepted the South's segregation policies. This acceptance was viewed as sufficiently solving the race problem. Many southerners did not develop elaborate justifications for segregation but generally assumed that segregation was compatible with Christianity and that intermarriage and social mixing were unacceptable. Many southern churchmen clearly taught Negro inferiority as an obvious truth.

A more liberal view on race relations was evident in the northern areas. Many northern church leaders identified the cause of the race problem as the ignorance and backwardness of Negroes and disliked their lower standard of living. Therefore liberal northerners enthusiastically supported educating Negroes, whereas southern churchmen were generally less convinced and more divided on the question of education's value. Liberal seminaries were often willing to open their doors to black clergymen. Many of these black Christians held conservative doctrinal positions on such questions as the inerrancy of Scripture. This, of course, was a problem for conservative students who were taught liberal positions, but the black clergymen had little choice because conservative seminaries, in the North or the South, would not admit blacks.

The large migration of blacks to the North caused racial tensions to peak and revealed a northern Christian prejudice that had not been evident formerly. White churches, which had allowed small numbers of blacks to attend and even participate in their services in the 1870s and 1880s, were not as welcoming of blacks in the 1890s and beyond. As the number of blacks attending a church increased, white members began to encourage them to find another place of worship. In Harlem, as the Negro population increased, many white churches informed their black members that they were no longer welcome and that they should join one of the black churches that was moving into their area.[12]

One specific example of this new tension occurred during the Sunday morning service on September 15, 1929, at Saint Matthew's Episcopal Church in Brooklyn, New York. The southern-born and educated rector, Rev. William Blackshear, read a section from the church bulletin before he began the sermon. In his congregation that morning there were a few Negroes who heard him:

> The Episcopal Church provides churches for Negroes. Several of these churches are within easy reach of this locality. They are in need of the loyal support of all true Negro churchmen; therefore, the rector of this parish discourages the attendance or membership in this church of members of that race.

His comments may have been precipitated by the growing number of Negroes in the community and the growing number of Negro visitors to the church. The next week the rector justified his actions by stating, "Although Christ preached love for all, there were times when even Christ refused the company of certain people."[13]

World War I

By the beginning of World War I segregation was the dominant characteristic of churches in the North and in the South. In most denominations there were no church laws that excluded Negroes from local white churches nor any laws prohibiting black ministers from having a predominantly white congregation. The main impediment was that social segregation had come to be accepted as the norm for the proper practicing of Christianity. It would have been shockingly absurd to assign or ask Negroes to serve as pastors of local white congregations where they would normally be shunned.

On the denominational level there was great variation in the participation and acceptance of Negroes at national conferences in the North and the South. The blacks who attended these denominational conferences were primarily there to represent the work that was occurring among their people. And, of course, these Negro participants faced the challenge of finding hotels that would accept them.

The Pentecostal Movement

A major positive development in race relations in Christianity involved the origin of the modern Pentecostal movement in the United States at the Azusa Street revival in Los Angeles, 1906–1909. The leader of the movement was William J. Seymour, a black Holiness preacher. Both blacks and whites of the Holiness movement were drawn to the Azusa Street revival. Therefore black Pentecostals trace their origin, unlike blacks of other mainline denominations, to a movement initiated by a black minister. Black Pentecostals also have the distinction of seeing their movement begin as an interracial movement from which whites later separated.[14]

While attending the Azusa Street revival in 1907 for five weeks, Charles Harrison Mason, the founder of a primarily black Holiness denomination in Mississippi named the Church of God in Christ (COGIC), and other elders were baptized "with the Holy Ghost and fire," which was manifested by their speaking in tongues. This group of men returned home and urged their church and denomination to implement the doctrine and practice of the baptism of the Holy Spirit. The general assembly of COGIC was divided in its views of the legitimacy of the doctrine of baptism of the Holy Ghost, and the majority rejected it. The two groups divided to form a non-Pentecostal group, which became the Church of Christ (Holiness), U.S.A., and another group that followed Mason and advocated speaking in tongues. Mason's group later won legal rights to the name Church of God in Christ, its corporate status, and most of the original body's property. Because COGIC was the only incorporated Pentecostal body in existence from 1907 to 1914, it was also the only church authority with which independent white Pentecostals were able to affiliate for legitimacy. For this reason many white ministers were ordained by Mason and officially became COGIC ministers.[15]

This was an unprecedented period in American evangelical history as white and black believers coexisted under a denomination that was headed by a black leader. Mason was dedicated to the belief that Christianity must be allowed to break the social boundaries that divided the races. Mason's work is noteworthy since its tenure was from the end of the Civil War through the "red summer of 1919" when social hatred was at its height.[16] Mason's desire to see people come to the Lord caused him to send evangelists to accompany the northern migration of blacks, which spread the denomination into metropolitan areas of New York, Philadelphia, Detroit, and Chicago. The interracial ministry of Mason in this racially tense period of history was so counter to the world's experience that the Federal Bureau of Investigation (FBI) had him under official nationwide surveillance. To guarantee the success of the surveillance, the FBI worked closely with the War Department, the Justice Department, and local police in many cities to document Mason's travels as he oversaw various COGIC ministries across the nation.

But the demands of a segregated society caused the Pentecostal movement to succumb and divide along racial lines. The white clergy who were ordained by Mason left the COGIC denomination to form what would later become the largest white Pentecostal denomination, the Assemblies of God, in 1914. By 1924 the brief interracial period among black and white Pentecostals had ended.

Interest in Social Action

The 1920s were difficult years for minority groups. The end of World War I brought an end to the idealism of the war period and ushered in a time of prosperity for the country. Social Christianity, which had grown in popularity before the war, lost a large part of its following as the focus was once again shifted by many churchmen solely to the preaching of Christ crucified. This was also a period when the church became divided by the struggle between modernists and fundamentalists. Although fundamentalists did not oppose the idea that Christianity needed to address social problems, they often opposed the advocates of the social gospel who were linked with the modernists. Unfortunately neither group really gave much consideration to Christianity's role in addressing the racial problem in America.

Despite a lack of focus on race relations by white evangelical church leaders, an interest in ministering to black people developed among white churchwomen in the 1920s. Many of them had been involved in Negro welfare work since 1910 and simply expanded their activities in the 1920s. Women, especially those in the Methodist and Presbyterian denominations, during this period enthusiastically studied the race problem, organized into groups, and knew enough individuals in the Negro community—Negro servants and workers in their homes—to be aware of their needs and to work to address those needs. Because white women were honored and protected in society, especially in southern society, they were shielded from criticism and reprisal, which allowed them to act boldly, even to the point of encouraging and participating in an interracial movement.

In the 1920s the interracial movement within denominations was fostered in the North, primarily through Congregationalists, and in the South, especially through Methodist women. The interracial movement sought to make life better for Negroes by eradicating lynching, securing equal public facilities for Negroes, and portraying them favorably in the media. Both clergy and laypeople of both races participated in these groups in the North and the South. In many respects the movement in the South was more active than its counterpart in the North. This active focus on race problems in the 1920s was aborted during the Great Depression (1930–1940) as most churches curtailed their program for Negro evangelism and education and concentrated on their own needs.

World War II and Beyond

The next major period in race relations extended from 1941 to 1954. With the end of World War II some American evangelicals began to question the racist policies in America that resembled the racist policies we fought to overthrow in Europe. Another factor in this period that led to a questioning of America's segregation policies was the return from other countries of evangelical missionaries who were convinced that a Jim Crow God could not win converts to Christianity in the nonwhite mission fields where they labored. Such a God was hard to promote to people groups influenced by nationalism and communism. Still, these concerns were not enough to change the American view that segregated churches were natural. Specific instances, in the North and the South, of blacks and whites worshiping together continued to be the rare exception.

Sociologist Frank Loescher conducted a survey of nearly eighteen thousand churches from various denominations in 1946 and estimated that eight thousand Negroes in the whole country were in churches with mixed membership. This figure was less than one-tenth of one percent of Negro Protestants. Most of these churches were in the North or West, notably in New England and in such states as New York, New Jersey, Pennsylvania, and California. It was very rare to have Negro members in white churches in the border regions or in the South. If there were Negro members in white churches of these regions, they were not well integrated into the social life of the church.

Loescher also found that one of the major obstacles to desegregation in the local churches in the North was the residential pattern. Yet even in neighborhoods that were undergoing racial transition, he could not find one white church that had an "open" membership policy. Only as Negroes became the majority in communities did membership in local white churches become open. He noted that the Protestant pattern was to resist the "Negro invasion" until the transition was complete, then to sell the property to a Negro church. His study led him to conclude, "Protestantism, by its policies and practices, far from helping to integrate the Negro in American life, is actually contributing to the segregation of Negro Americans."[17]

Various churches attempted different approaches to achieve racially inclusive churches. There was an interdenominational venture to intentionally create interracial churches; some white churches stayed in a transitioning neighborhood and opened their doors to their Negro neighbors; Negro and white congregations combined to form interracial congregations; there were Negro and white clergy who occasionally swapped pulpits; and Negro and white congregations worshiped together on a Race Relations Sunday. Race Relations Sunday was an established program begun by the Federal Council of Churches in 1922. By the end of the 1940s most Protestant denominations, with the exception of the southern Presbyterians, were calling for racial inclusion in their denominations. One rallying cry for the endeavor was for a "non-segregated church in a non-segregated society."[18]

Still, the movement toward a racially inclusive church continued to be a slow process. The northern Presbyterian Church was one of the first denominations to vote in their general assembly to end segregation in their churches and to support the Supreme Court's decision on school segregation. They took that step in 1954, the beginning of the next historical stage in race relations.

A Vision of Racial Reconciliation

Way before the idea of racial reconciliation was even considered by most people, Dr. Clarence Jordan was committed to it, even to the point of risking his life and the lives of his family. Born and raised in Georgia, Clarence Jordan was an exceptional individual who combined scholarship and Christian discipleship to impact his society for the sake of the ministry of racial reconciliation. Jordan graduated from the University of Georgia with a bachelors degree in agriculture and later earned a master of theology and Ph.D. degree in New Testament Greek from Southern Baptist Seminary in Louisville, Kentucky. Yet his scholarship was clearly submitted to his intense commitment to see the teachings of Jesus taken seriously in daily life.

In November 1942 Jordan's commitment was evidenced when he and his wife, Florence, and another white couple, Martin and Mabel England, moved to a 440-acre farm in Sumter County, near Americus, Georgia. The intent of their move was to start an interracial community in which blacks and whites would live and work together amid the poverty and racism of the rural South.

The farm was named Koinonia, a Greek word used in Acts to describe the early church. It means fellowship or community. The Jordans and Englands determined to accomplish their goal by living according to three principles:

1. All humankind are related under God's parenthood.
2. Love (pacifism) is the alternative to violence.
3. They would share all their possessions.

Through Bible studies with their neighbors, primarily children at first, interracial friendships began to develop, and a small residential community began to fellowship together over meals and work. Such interracial communion, however, was not acceptable in the South, and if it had not been for God's protection and Jordan's quick wit, the new endeavor would have ended quickly.

A group of men came to the farm. Their spokesman said to Clarence, "We're from the Ku Klux Klan and we don't allow the sun to set on people who eat with niggers." Clarence glanced over at the western sky and noticed that the sun was creeping low. He thought a bit, swallowed a few times, and suddenly reached out, grabbed the man's hand, and started pumping away, saying, "Why, I just graduated from Southern Baptist Seminary, and they told us there about folks who had power over the sun, but I never hoped to meet one here in Sumter County." They all laughed, and nobody noticed that the sun had slipped down below the horizon.[19]

Tragically, the Jordans' commitment to racial equality and the growth of the Koinonia community were taken more seriously by the local Southern Baptist Church where they had been members for eight years. The church excommunicated them in 1950 because of their views on racial equality.[20]

Within the interracial community these neighbors lived, ate meals, farmed, and attended Bible studies and youth camps together. Koinonia remained committed to nonviolence and racial equality even though during the 1950s and 1960s, the surrounding white community's wrath against them was expressed through death threats, shots fired into their homes, firebombs, Ku Klux Klan rallies, a grand jury summons, accusations of Communist ties, property damages, abuse of their children at school, and economic boycotts—boycotting their farm produce and refusing to sell anything to them.

Through these long and challenging years of hard labor, the scholar Jordan gave a gift to Koinonia and to Christianity in America. His gift was in the form of the *Cotton Patch* version of the New Testament Scriptures, which was his translation of the New Testament Greek into the language of twentieth-century America, with a Southern accent. Clarence Jordan was also instrumental in inspiring Millard and Linda Fuller to begin in 1976 the ministry that is known today as Habitat for Humanity.

Clarence Jordan died in 1969, but today his dream continues to be pursued through the strong ministry of Koinonia Partners (the present name of the Koinonia ministries, which includes housing construction for those who cannot afford it, a farm, and an interracial community of residents and volunteers), which continues to challenge its local white community. A fruit of Koinonia's challenge has been manifested in some of the lives of young people whose parents participated in the oppression of Koinonia in years past. Florence Jordan says she has been visited on several occasions by students who admitted to having harassed her children while they were in school together. On each occasion these young people came to apologize and to communicate their esteem for the people of Koinonia.[21]

THREE

SEPARATE
AND ALARMED

The Civil Rights movement was a watershed in black and white relations in the United States. This period that began in 1954 and peaked out in the early 1970s caused as much tension in the evangelical church as it did in society at large. The movement was empowered by black churches but opposed by most white churches.

The modern Civil Rights movement began on May 17, 1954, with the Supreme Court's ruling that segregated public schools were unconstitutional in the *Brown v. Board of Education* case. Counter to the South's argument, the Supreme Court ruled that segregation was a denial of equal protection of the law and this destroyed the legal foundations for segregation in the South.[1] Encouraged by this momentous decision, blacks were inspired to take action. The Supreme Court ruling so motivated Thurgood Marshall, the young NAACP attorney who argued the case before the Supreme Court, that he predicted that America would be totally integrated by 1963—the one hundredth anniversary of the Emancipation Proclamation.[2]

The Role of the Black Church

The prominent role of the Black Church in the African American community's fight for freedom in previous decades did not change during this period. The 1954 Supreme Court decision was evidence of this. The key person in the case that desegregated education in America was a black minister. The Reverend Oliver Leon Brown of the St. Mark's African Methodist Episcopal Church in Topeka, Kansas, brought the suit against the board of education on behalf of his nine-year-old daughter, Linda, and all other black children who were hindered by segregation in the public school system.

Another evidence of the Black Church's role began on December 1, 1955, when seamstress Rosa Parks stepped on a bus in downtown Montgomery, Alabama, and refused to give up her seat to a white person. There had been other women who were removed from buses for not giving up their seats to whites, but community leaders did not believe that these women had the personal or social characteristics needed to rally the black community to action. These community leaders believed that the plaintiff who could successfully challenge the bus company had to be above reproach for the religious, conservative black community to embrace her. And the support and influence of the city's powerful black churches were critical for rallying Montgomery's black community to action against the injustices of the bus company. One of the injustices that angered blacks most was the pay and leave practice of some bus drivers. Blacks were often forced to pay at the front of the bus but then enter the bus through the rear door. It had become the practice of some bus drivers to leave after the Negro patrons had paid their fare at the front but had not had time to board the bus through the rear door. Mrs. Parks had the personal and moral character necessary to galvanize the community around her stand. And galvanized they were, as 50,000 blacks stayed off buses for 381 days at the risk of losing jobs and even their lives.[3]

At the very heart of this great event was the Black Church and its representatives. Pastors such as Martin Luther King Jr. and Ralph Abernathy provided strong leadership, and church organizations such as the Women's Political Council of Montgomery provided the organization and support network. Two years after the beginning of the boycott, Dr. King organized the Southern Christian Leadership Conference as the political arm of the Black Church to support the national goals of the movement. The Southern Christian Leadership Conference gave direction to local church involvement. In turn hundreds of black clergy and their congregations made extraordinary sacrifices to support the cause and pursue freedom.

The bus boycott was a success but it was uncertain if the larger goals of the Civil Rights movement under the leadership of Dr. King could be achieved. Never before had a clear underdog—African Americans were only 10 to 12 percent of the population—been able to use the nonviolence method to bring about a change in society. The nonviolence method had been used by Mahatma Gandhi in India and would later be used by Desmond Tutu in South Africa, but these oppressed racial groups were clearly the majority in their countries. In the United States, on the other hand, African Americans never had the large numbers necessary to move the opposition government to action. Therefore it was essential that African Americans begin to view their fight as a legitimate moral cause. Through the communication of white American culture, blacks had adopted a sense of inferiority, which kept them from uniting to oppose societal or institutionalized racism. The first goal of the movement was to instill pride in blacks as a people and to create in them a sense of unity that would result in a social movement aimed at fighting the wrongs of racism.

The Role of the White Church

During the early period of the Civil Rights movement, most whites in the North and the South were uncertain as to the correctness of the movement. Most southerners were caught off guard because they thought that their "coloreds" were content with the way things were. They viewed this movement as the result of northern blacks coming South and stirring things up. Most northerners saw the movement as needed in the South but misguided when it moved northward to address issues in the North. Racism, they believed, was a southern issue.[4]

Unfortunately white evangelical, and especially white fundamentalist, Christians did not support the movement for three major reasons. First, because most whites were disconnected from the daily lives and struggles of blacks, they could not understand the urgency of eliminating racism and segregation's effects on the black community. Second, most whites had come to view the segregation that existed in Christianity as normal and acceptable. The comment of one member of a Gulfport, Mississippi, Mennonite church in the 1950s exemplifies this: "If a Negro were truly Christian, they would not come to our church. If they found out that their presence would be offensive to people, they would not come so as not to offend them."[5] Third, many whites misunderstood Dr. King and therefore viewed him with suspicion. They were quick to believe that he was a communist and a liberal theologian and they were unable to hear his call for Christian love to overcome the evil of racism in America. The absence of Bible-believing churches from the list of churches supporting him and the movement was certainly a source of disappointment to Dr. King. Evangelicals as a whole never came to recognize the importance of the Civil Rights movement nor their need to be involved in it. This absence became an issue of division between black and white evangelicals that continues today.

Yet changing racial attitudes within evangelicalism, though slow, were already in motion. In June 1954 at the Southern Baptist Convention's annual meeting in St. Louis, a resolution strongly supporting the Supreme Court's school desegregation ruling was brought to the floor. Many of the 1,900 southern delegates were shocked and the resolution seemed to be heading for clear defeat. But then Dr. Jesse Burton Weatherspoon, a highly esteemed professor at Southern Baptist Seminary at Louisville, Kentucky, moved to the speaker's stand and stated, "We have over our heads the banner, 'Forward With Jesus Christ.' Our only question is, what is the most Christian thing to do? If we withdraw this motion, we will say to the people of the United States, count Southern Baptists out in this matter of equal justice for all. I do not believe we want to say that." The resolution was adopted by a strong majority.[6]

In 1957 prominent evangelical Billy Graham decided to add Howard Jones, a black pastor and evangelist, to his crusade team. Graham's decision to have a black person on his team was based on the small African American turnout at his sixty-eight-day crusade in New York's Madison Square Garden in 1957. From this experience Graham recommitted himself to achieving the pledge he had made after the 1954 *Brown v. Board of Education* decision to never have another segregated crusade. Although Graham had already integrated his staff with the addition of a gifted preacher from India, his decision to add a black person to his staff was quickly met with warnings by white clergy and threats to cut off support. Of these early days of integration on Graham's team, Jones stated, "I was overwhelmed with a sense of loneliness. The stares, the people muttering under their voices. . . . I remember sitting on the crusade platform on various occasions with empty seats next to me because some white crusade participants had decided to sit on the other side of the stage."[7]

From Peace to Power

The grueling struggle against racism forged by the Civil Rights movement resulted in major civil rights legislation, the Civil Rights Act of 1964, and finally the Voting Rights Act of 1965, which gave blacks the right to vote. But these achievements were not sufficient for many black activists who believed that race would continue to determine an individual's life chances in America.[8] For this reason a more radical movement arose, which was seen most dramatically in the Black Panthers. The Panthers' growing popularity among young black Americans fulfilled the prophecy of Dr. Martin Luther King Jr.: "Those who make a peaceful resolution impossible, will make a violent revolution inevitable." The rallying cry of this radical edge was "Black Power," which was a very vague and fluid concept that was frequently interpreted as a call to separatism but was really a desire to see blacks take control of their own destiny.

The formulators of this concept, Stokely Carmichael and Charles V. Hamilton, defined black power as the need for black people to unite, recognize their heritage, recognize that their heritage is a proud and noble one, build a sense of community, define their own goals, be actively involved in the decisions and actions that lead to the accomplishment of those goals, lead their own organizations, and support those organizations. Black power was a call to reject the racist institutions and values of American society. They wrote that the fundamental premise on which the concept of black power rests is "Before a group can enter the open society, it must first close ranks."[9]

A key figure in drawing attention from the Civil Rights movement to the black power movement was Malcolm X. He argued that the dependency of blacks on white America was the cause of their troubles and the answer was for them to separate in order to build their own nation within a nation. Clearly those who advocated black power did not see integration as a *goal* of their movement that would result in political power and equality. Rather, they saw integration as a *result* of their movement's having gained political power and equality through self-empowerment. For the white community, even for its liberal fringe, this radical approach to race relations generated great alarm.

White evangelical churches were probably even more alarmed than the general public by the strident cries and behavior of those who advocated "Black Power." And alarm seemed valid in the late sixties when young blacks entered white evangelical churches with the intent of disrupting services and showing their contempt for church policy that prohibited blacks from becoming members. There was a domino effect as churches panicked and, fearing that their services might be disrupted, blocked all blacks from attending their churches. I am aware of four churches, three in the Midwest and one in the South, that have a very bad reputation among their African American neighbors because of the "precautionary steps" they took during these turbulent years.

Black evangelicals were also challenged during this period about their commitment to the improvement of the lives of African Americans. The black power movement created great skepticism about the relevance of black evangelicals and their gospel to the lives of African Americans. In one of his first sermons Malcolm X stated that the Christianity of whites "brainwashed" blacks into focusing on God's promise of a kingdom to come rather than on God's desire to see our present conditions changed.[10] Black evangelicals became aware that their white affiliations would result in close scrutiny and possible criticism concerning their allegiance to the black community. To combat such criticism, many black church leaders chose to emphasize the importance of black culture over the need for reconciliation with whites.

By the end of this period, race relations had become an issue that caused divisions among black Christians as it had already caused among white Christians. One group of black Christians sought collaboration and fellowship with white Christians, even joining white churches. Another group of black Christians developed a strong desire to revel in the rich religious-cultural traditions that had been developed throughout their experience in America.

There seemed to be three fundamental reasons that prevented black Christians from participating in a ministry of racial reconciliation:

1. The continued distrust many black Christians had of whites because of the white Christian community's centuries of quiet neglect
2. The fear that involvement in a ministry of racial reconciliation would result in blacks having to give up their religious-cultural traditions to accommodate white religious-cultural preferences
3. Concern that black religious leaders would have to forfeit their position as leaders to serve under whites in interracial ministry endeavors

Overall, this period continued to reveal that the Christian community lagged behind the larger society in progress toward improving black and white relations in the United States.

FOUR

SEPARATE BUT EVANGELICAL

The societal changes that were brought about by the Civil Rights movement in the sixties set the stage for significant events in the contemporary period. Slowly white evangelicals are coming to realize and acknowledge their underestimation of racial discrimination and their failure to be actively involved in the Civil Rights movement. They are learning to love and minister impartially. Black Christians are being freed from the societal restraints that have hindered their leading, or in some cases even being involved in, major Christian organizations. Yet our examination of this period reveals that race continues to play a prominent role in Christianity at the beginning of the twenty-first century.

The 1970s

In the aftermath of the sixties, the great changes that were brought about by the Civil Rights movement were only minimally felt in evangelical Christianity. To many white Christians the Civil Rights movement was another example of the disrespectful spirit toward authority that was evident in the sixties. To these individuals the limited benefits of the movement were overshadowed by its disdain for law and order and its emphasis on social reform rather than on spiritual issues. White evangelical Christians continued to consider race a nonissue and to give their full attention to evangelism and to fulfilling the Great Commission. There was a sigh of relief that the decade of the sixties with its riots and demonstrations was now over.

The perspective was different for black Christians who came out of this period emboldened by the achievements of the Civil Rights movement but disappointed by the inability of white Christians to see the importance of racial issues. For most black Christians the changes of the sixties were only the beginning of reforms that had to be boldly continued in the seventies. For most members of both groups, however, racial reconciliation was not a priority. Yet there were a few who had caught this vision.

Christian Leaders of Racial Reconciliation

One voice speaking out for racial reconciliation was that of black evangelist Tom Skinner. In the 1970s Skinner was viewed as an ambassador to white evangelicals as he spoke boldly in such settings as Urbana '70 and through such mediums as his weekly radio program. He was a black evangelical who spoke to both races about the need for racial reconciliation. He challenged blacks to see that racial reconciliation was an issue that was not just for whites. Skinner desired to see black evangelicals realize their place in God's kingdom agenda and to join with whites in bringing that kingdom agenda to impact the world. He challenged whites with their responsibility to preach and live out the message of the gospel so that it would rightly impact the black community. It was not enough for whites to preach that the gospel was the answer for the inner city if they did not become personally involved in taking the gospel to these areas. In the period from 1969 to 1973 the audience at Skinner's crusades was 60 percent white and 40 percent black. A major reason for this crossover was Skinner's familiarity with white evangelicalism through his education. Still, his bold and socially relevant interpretation of the Scriptures also made him a strong defender of the gospel against the attacks of black power advocates.

John Perkins was another strong advocate of the need for the reconciliation of whites and blacks. Perkins had lived his life based on the importance of reconciliation for the proper representation of the gospel. When asked in a 1982 *Christianity Today* article about the key to his success in developing black leaders, Perkins stated, "Because of white involvement; I believe reconciliation is the key to the gospel. Anyone should feel confident he can win anyone to Jesus Christ. This requires black leadership. It also requires white leadership that will facilitate the development of black leadership."[1] Perkins's life and actions have been strong testimonies to his commitment to the ministry of racial reconciliation.

The life and actions of Billy Graham have also strongly advocated racial reconciliation in the body of Christ. It was Graham who observed, "the most segregated hour of the week is still 11 o'clock Sunday morning," in a 1960 *Reader's Digest* article titled "Why Don't Our Churches Practice the Brotherhood They Preach?"[2] Graham was a close friend of Dr. King, whom he called "Mike" at the Civil Rights leader's request, and would use his insights to later help change the position on race of the Southern Baptist Convention, of which he is a member. In 1970 Graham's pastor and Southern Baptist Convention president W. A. Criswell, pastor of the prominent First Baptist Church of Dallas, admitted in his book *Look Up, Brother!* that, although his church had always permitted blacks to attend and participate in the life of the church and its school, they had never made a public statement on race. One reason for that was Criswell's own belief, which had undergone a change.

In fact, it had been my stated persuasion that we ought to go our separate ways, the colored community and the white community, the colored church and the white church, the black Christian and the white Christian. But as I prayed, searched the Holy Scripture, preached the gospel, and worked with our people, I came to the profound conclusion that to separate by coercion the body of Christ on the basis of skin pigmentation was unthinkable, unchristian, and unacceptable to God.[3]

Racism Continues

These advocates of racial reconciliation notwithstanding, this early period of the new decade continued to show evidences of racism's presence in American Christianity. In 1971 the Internal Revenue Service (IRS) denied tax-exempt status to about a hundred private schools, including Christian schools, in the United States that discriminated on the basis of race. One of the most prominent Christian schools involved was Bob Jones University, which, along with a group of Christian schools in North Carolina, challenged the decision of the IRS, fighting it until the case came before the Supreme Court. From the year of the suit to the Supreme Court's final ruling in 1983, the ugly head of racism in Christianity was prominently displayed in the national media.[4] During this period, America learned that not until 1975 were blacks first admitted to Bob Jones University. Despite this change in policy, interracial dating by students and faculty continued to be prohibited, and those involved in interracial marriages could not attend the university. These prohibitions were surprising since the school had fewer than twelve blacks among its six thousand students in 1982. The ban on interracial dating was finally lifted on March 3, 2000, several weeks after presidential candidate George W. Bush delivered a speech at the school. This focused the spotlight of the national media on the school's position on interracial dating and on other issues, which quickly engendered nationwide condemnation.[5] Still, Bob Jones's policies were more progressive than those of the Christian schools that partnered with the university in its Supreme Court case, for blacks were still not allowed admission to these schools in 1983.

The Supreme Court ruled in 1983 that Bob Jones University and those schools that chose not to change their racial policies could not receive the government's tax-exempt status. Many white evangelicals, although opposing the racially discriminatory policies of Bob Jones University, came out in public support of the university because the ruling might eventually have a negative impact on religious freedom and on the rights of thousands of secular and religious nonprofit groups. But to many blacks, the opposition to the ruling was seen as another clear example of the failure of white Christians to oppose racism and to live out the biblical principles they espoused.

The 1980s

The wedge that had been driven between black and white Christians in America because of the apparent indifference of whites to the injustices endured daily by blacks was driven even more securely in place during the 1980s. The two groups usually were at opposite poles on political issues, such as the position of the United States on South Africa and its policy of apartheid and the social and economic policies of the Reagan administration. Many blacks perceived these policies as evidence of the administration's social justice insensitivity.

One of the most important issues to African Americans in the 1980s was that of South Africa and the belief that the United States government should place sanctions on that country as long as it held to its policy of apartheid. This issue was especially important to African Americans because of their own history and their determination that our government should not support racism in Africa. The battle over this issue broke along party lines as the Republican Party, which was viewed by many white evangelical Christians as their hope for America's moral renewal, opposed sanctions, while Democrats, the party to which most blacks belonged and considered an advocate for their cause since the Civil Rights movement, supported their use. The Reagan administration adopted a policy of "constructive engagement," which sought to influence the South African government through negotiation. But under pressure, Reagan later changed his policy to "active, constructive engagement," which progressively sought to use sanctions to obtain political change. Although a political issue, the evangelical community was soon focused on its debate.

As Jerry Falwell, founder and prominent representative of the Moral Majority, voiced his opposition to sanctions, many African Americans saw it as another indication of the lack of sensitivity that white evangelicals had to the wrongs of racism. It was an emotional issue. Clarence Hilliard, a Chicago pastor and resolutions chairman of the National Black Evangelical Association (NBEA), made this clear when he said, "White evangelicals will either have to take a stand against him [Falwell] or be identified with him. That may not be too promising, because white evangelicals have a tendency to be silent on these kinds of things."[6]

The eighties would continue to reveal a strong line of conflict that ran along racial and political affiliations. One issue that revealed the stark difference in perspective between the races was abortion. The promise of Republican conservatives that this issue would become a key focus when they obtained political power fostered abortion's rise to its position as the moral issue of the decade. Although most African Americans were pro-life, they were not actively involved in the pro-life movement's opposition to abortion. There are two fundamental reasons for the absence of African Americans in this movement. First, many African Americans believe that the pro-life movement has improperly focused all of its attention on the unborn, while ignoring the life needs of the unemployed, homeless, and poor. Although noting the importance of ending abortion, many African Americans did not see it as the most important social issue of the eighties. Second, African Americans remembered the dearth of white evangelicals in the fight for justice during the Civil Rights movement. Now these white evangelicals were giving themselves wholeheartedly to the pro-life movement, and black evangelicals found the inconsistency hard to accept. The strong disagreement in perspective was evident but an even stronger mistrust by African Americans of their white brethren was also very real. So strong was this mistrust of the pro-life agenda that many black evangelicals have openly wondered if there would even be such a movement if abortions were only occurring to black babies.

Mistrust between black and white evangelicals became more and more palpable as the eighties progressed. Midway through the decade a significant oversight with racial overtones seemed to epitomize the deep gulf that had developed. The Houston '85 National Convocation on Evangelizing Ethnic America was an international conference sponsored by the North American Lausanne Committee for World Evangelization. Conference organizers did not invite African Americans to plan or even attend the conference. The leaders of the Houston Convocation justified their actions by stating that the conference was for non-English-speaking minorities. Many African Americans, on the other hand, perceived it as just another oversight of black Christians by white evangelicals. In response, black evangelical leaders organized their own conference, which met in Atlanta in 1988, on evangelizing black America. Unfortunately, this incident mirrored the nature of the relationship between black and white evangelicals in the 1980s. Their agenda and goals continued to be characterized by unity in calling but were separate in implementation.

The 1990s

The final decade of the twentieth century was a momentous period in American race relations that presented both challenges and triumphs for this cause. The decade was not very old when race took center stage as the horrific image of white police officers beating a fallen, unarmed black motorist was repeatedly flashed over the television screens of millions of Americans. When the four police officers were later acquitted in 1992 for the videotaped beating, Americans witnessed the most costly civil disorder of the twentieth century in the United States. More than ten thousand people were arrested, more than fifty people were killed, and property damage exceeded one billion dollars during riots in South Central Los Angeles. Rioting also erupted in other large cities across the country.

Like the urban riots of the 1960s, the Los Angeles riot was clearly racially motivated, but unlike those earlier riots, this one revealed the great extent to which race continued to divide Americans. Although the riot's participants included blacks, whites, Latinos, and Asian Americans, there was indication that racial hostilities within and between these groups prevailed.[7] An image that was more horrific than that of the Rodney King beating was the brutal bludgeoning during the riot of white truck driver Reginald Denney in a senseless act of blind retaliation by black youths.[8]

Three years later the country was once again shaken by another racially charged event as O. J. Simpson was acquitted of the double murders of his former wife, Nicole Simpson, and her friend Ronald Goldman. The reponse to the verdict further revealed the deep racial divide that existed in America as many African Americans jubilantly rejoiced while many whites slumped in shock and anger. The racial split was even evident in Simpson's defense team as white attorney Robert Shapiro chided his colleagues for making race a part of their defense strategy.

Three weeks after this event Nation of Islam leader Louis Farrakhan's call for a Million Man March on Washington, D.C., was answered by at least four hundred thousand black men. These two events led Boston pastor Eugene Rivers to conclude that Americans were descending into "a state of psychological apartheid."[9] Unfortunately the racial separation evident in American society was also very apparent in evangelical Christianity.

Even in the nineties America's neighborhood churches remained segregated. America's social patterns were the primary reason for this: Its neighborhoods remained segregated, hindering efforts at racial reconciliation.

Research in the early nineties showed that evangelical Christian organizations still did not have a good representation of blacks as employees. These organizations had even fewer blacks in management positions. The primary reason for this limited representation was the lack of contact between minority believers, many of whom were located in urban areas, and evangelical organizations, many of which were located in suburban areas.

There was also a low number of blacks attending Christian schools and colleges, a disheartening fact since many of these schools were located in or near urban areas.

Progress in Racial Reconciliation

Although the decade found black and white Christians still separated in most areas of their lives, this was a decade of major advances in respect to reconciliation. One movement that would greatly affect the nature of race relations in Christianity through its example was the Promise Keepers movement. During its 1991 conference, Promise Keepers founder Bill McCartney stated that he looked out on the University of Colorado's Folsom Stadium, which at that time held four thousand men, and was hit by the realization that the group was overwhelmingly white. "The absence of men of color somehow hit me between the eyes, and in that moment, the Spirit of God clearly said to my spirit, 'You can fill that stadium, but if men of other races aren't there, I won't be there, either.'"[10] Promise Keepers has, since that point, made a conscious and committed effort to become racially diverse. Their commitment is evident in the culturally diverse musical styles used for worship, the inclusion of various ethnic speakers, and the hiring of minority staff and appointment of people of color to the board. In 1995 African American pastor Phillip Porter was appointed as Promise Keepers's board chairman.

In February 1995 Promise Keepers announced their intention to have one hundred thousand pastors attend a Promise Keepers conference in Atlanta. This pastors' event was undertaken on the premise that if reconciliation was going to happen in the church, it would have to start among God's leaders. Unfortunately the number of African Americans attending Promise Keepers rallies continues to be smaller than the ministry desires and Bill McCartney has stated that the racial message continues to challenge the ministry's attendance and financial support by white men.

Three Important Events

After the Los Angeles riots, many churches in the Los Angeles area joined together to meet the needs of those affected by the riot. For many this was their first experience in cross-cultural ministry, which should be surprising for churches in Los Angeles in the 1990s. But to many African American leaders, it's not at all surprising. In 1992 the editors of *Christianity Today* had conversations with prominent African American Christian leaders across the country. These conversations revealed the feelings of frustration that these leaders felt in respect to the outlook of many white evangelicals. William H. Bentley, president of the National Black Evangelical Association (NBEA), criticized the attitude of whites who dominated the predominantly white National

Association of Evangelicals (NAE), "It holds itself as white first and Christian second. . . . White supremacy—they would shrink from being called that. But they practice it. They practice it like all white people."[11] William Pannell believes that most of the steps to change have to be taken by white Christians: "It's the white culture's problem, not ours." He noted that white evanglicals must truly repent and "Until something like that happens, I don't envision black evangelicals taking their white counterparts seriously."[12]

A year later *Christianity Today* asked forty-one prominent African American Christian leaders, most of them evangelicals, to answer the question, "What do you want your white evangelical brothers and sisters to hear right now?" They included a selection of these responses and summarized them as, "The words are personal and emotional, strong and shocking. Some are hopeful, but most are angry."[13] In this article evangelical social activist John Perkins stated:

> Something is wrong at the root of American evangelicalism. I believe we have lost the focus of the gospel—God's reconciling power, which is unique to Christianity—and have substituted church growth. We have learned to reproduce the church without the message. It is no longer a message that transforms.[14]

That same year Billy Graham stated:

> Racial and ethnic hostility is the foremost social problem facing our world today. . . . Racism—in the world and in the church—is one of the greatest barriers to world evangelization. Racial and ethnic hatred is a sin, we need to label it as such.[15]

But in the years that followed three major racial reconciliation events occurred.

Reconciliation in the Pentecostal Church

In October 1994 leaders of twenty-one white Pentecostal groups gathered in Memphis for three days of meetings to reconcile themselves, and the Christians they represented, to the African American representatives of the Church of God in Christ, which is based in Memphis. The gathering was sponsored by the Pentecostal Fellowship of North America (PFNA), which began in 1948 as a segregated group for white Pentecostal leaders. The board members of PFNA demonstrated their sincerity by dissolving their organization. A new interracial organization, the Pentecostal and Charismatic Churches of North America (PCCNA), was then formed and included top COGIC bishops. The group then elected COGIC Bishop Ithiel Clemmons as PCCNA's first chairperson. Clemmons is the first African American to hold such a prominent leadership position among white Pentecostals since C. H. Mason began ordaining white ministers in the early 1900s. The meetings were highlighted by other acts of reconciliation that included a black pastor's humbling himself to wash the feet of the white general superintendent of the Assemblies of God, and a white pastor doing the same to a black bishop of the Church of God in Christ. B. E. Underwood, head of the Pentecostal Holiness denomination, stated, "What a difference it would have made during the civil rights movement in America if all the children of the Pentecostal revival had stood together."[16]

The NEA and NBEA

In January 1995 the National Association of Evangelicals (NAE) and the National Black Evangelical Association (NBEA) held a special joint session to commit themselves to building racial harmony. The National Negro (later changed to Black) Evangelical Association was incorporated in 1964. The organization was founded because black evangelicals believed that social concerns, such as hunger, poverty, and racism, that were relevant to blacks were being excluded from the agenda of the predominantly white National Association of Evangelicals. Through the years some black evangelicals have called for a total disengagement from white evangelicals but others have argued that it was their responsibility to challenge white evangelical institutions and organizations to become socially engaged. The choice was made to continue an association with white evangelicals in the NAE and this helped bring about this momentous event in 1995.

At the meeting the process of reconciliation between these two groups began when the new executive director of the NAE, Don Argue, publicly confessed and repented of racism within the evangelical movement. In response, three African American leaders laid hands on Argue and prayed for him as he knelt before them. The prayer was for the breaking down of walls that existed between the races and for wisdom on how they should proceed in the future. Loaves of bread were then distributed to be symbolically broken together, followed by a time of praise and prayer. To continue the process of reconciliation, many attendees formed accountability relationships with individuals of another race and also participated in small-group discussions on how individuals and the organizations they represented could deepen relationships across racial lines.

In early 2000 the two organizations continue to exist as separate entities.

The Apology

The third event that had great impact on racial reconciliation was a historic apology by the Southern Baptist Convention at its 150th anniversary convention in 1995. The Southern Baptists apologized for their racist position in the 1800s that led them to form their own convention. The resolution in part states, "We apologize to all African Americans for condoning and/or perpetuating individual and systematic racism in our lifetime, and we genuinely repent of racism of which we have been guilty, whether consciously or unconsciously."[17]

Because the Southern Baptist Convention is the nation's largest Protestant denomination, its apology was noteworthy. After its inception in 1845 the denomination did not show any interest in having contact with blacks until 1951 when the first black church joined the convention. Later in 1954 they became the first denomination to support the Supreme Court's decision against public school segregation and in 1965 they began to observe a race relations day. Although many African Americans have not forgotten the early role of the Southern Baptists in race relations in the United States, it is clear that many blacks are moving beyond that history. Since 1989, when the denomination intentionally set out to start black churches, the Southern Baptists have planted an average of 150 black churches a year. The present trend of African American churches in the Southern Baptist Convention is significant as it now has more black churches than the third largest black Baptist denomination (the Progressive National Baptist Convention).[18]

Despite the progress made among Christians toward racial reconciliation, the journey will clearly be a long and tedious one. National cases of random racial violence by whites and blacks continue to show that American society has a long way to go before racial unity is fully achieved. Unfortunately the church of Jesus Christ has shown that it has not made much more progress than the society at large. Although many congregations in the United States have intentionally become cross-cultural, local churches continue to be the final territory of racial segregation in American society. As John Perkins states, "The church is segregated now because that's what we like. In [Martin Luther] King's era, churches were segregated because whites didn't want to be around blacks. Now it's two-sided. Today we both choose to be separate."[19]

STILL SEPARATE

There once was a town in which there lived two groups of people. One group wore black hats and the other group wore white hats. Although these two groups would come into contact with each other in various settings, such as at work and athletic events, they were hindered from having intimate interactions by a huge wall that ran between them. The wall had been built over a period of three hundred years and ran through every neighborhood, school, place of employment, recreational facility, and location in the town where the two groups could possibly come into contact with one another. The only locations along the wall where no contact was the norm were the churches. In the churches the wall totally divided the members of the two groups, keeping them on one side or the other.

For the black hats this wall had become a memorial that inspired solidarity and pride in their people's ability to make it through tremendous difficulties. There was no aesthetic beauty in this wall, for it was really quite ugly, even repulsive, but because of it, the black hats had achieved their unique culture and identity. For most black hats the wall had become such an expected part of their existence that they made their homes in its very shadow.

Most black hats believed that secret additions continued to be made to the wall by the white hats, and they often said, "Some things never change." Some had dedicated their lives to watching the wall to make sure that additions didn't continue to be made because, "You can never trust the white hats."

For the white hats this wall had become a deteriorating and embarrassing relic of an ancient time long past. They saw no beauty in the wall but reluctantly admitted that some of their ancestors assisted in its construction. Most would say that it had no effect on their present life situation or anyone else's, black hat or white hat. But it was hard for them to know. Most white hats had moved so far away from the wall that they couldn't see it in their day-to-day activities. They could see it only when they were forced to look for it, and they believed that the black hats took every opportunity to force them to do so. Most white hats believed that the recent additions to the wall didn't represent the will of the majority of white hats, but were erected by a few misguided wall gazers from their group. If the truth be known, most white hats would like to break the wall down and wipe its existence from the history books.

Of course, the town in the preceding scenario is America and the wall is the psychological and emotional separation that has resulted from almost four hundred years of racism in this country. Clearly the wall of America's race history continues to divide blacks and whites from experiencing intimate interactions because they have two different views of its impact on their relationship. For blacks the wall can never be forgiven and they dare not attempt to diminish its significance in daily interactions with white people. For whites the wall has been denounced and forgotten. They believe it is time to move on and they have. There is a standoff, and the gospel's message of forgiveness and reconciliation is the only answer to it.

The historical failure of the evangelical church in America to make the ministry of racial reconciliation a central component of its purpose is now limiting its ability to release the gospel's power to heal racial divisions. This is very sad, especially when such organizations as the military and the federal government are praised for their ability to integrate the races, bringing them into social contact within the context of their respective environments. We know, of course, that this kind of integration is not enough, because social contact does not guarantee that the hearts of individuals will be changed. The church must not only attempt to bring estranged people together but must also deal, as only the church can, with the issues that separated them. To do less is to create a cosmetic truce, a truce that is acknowledged but not applied. Such an approach covers up the issues, hoping that they will go away, but this approach cannot deal with the resultant damage brought about by centuries of abuse, hurt, and anger. Centuries of primarily negative interaction between the races have impacted American evangelicalism in countless ways. Here are four that I believe have been most damaging and that continue to debilitate black and white relations in the evangelical church: obstructive traditions, a superiority/inferiority struggle, a lack of trust, and a false sense of self-sufficiency.

Obstructive Traditions

There are various traditions that are held by both whites and blacks that obstruct or hinder racial reconciliation. For both groups these traditions have become associated with what it means to be a Christian. Like treasured family heirlooms these customs are guarded by the sacred chant, "This is what we're used to."

A news account that sadly echoes this chant, and reveals the extent to which racial reconciliation continues to be hindered, appeared in my local newspaper in March 1997. It was called, "Casting of Black Jesus Incites Tumult."[1] It seems that an eighty-two-year-old passion play tradition in Union

City, New Jersey, would be broken by the casting of a black man in the role of Jesus. This decision was quickly met with derogatory phone calls, cancellations from a number of groups, a request for one group's reservation to be switched to another date when an alternate cast that featured a white Jesus would be performing, and even a death threat! Can you imagine that? Quite possibly you can if you were raised with the image of an Anglo Saxon Jesus gracing your church bulletin covers, or his blue eyes looking down at you from the mural over the baptismal pool. There is nothing wrong with those memories or childhood images, unless they are taken to be the *only* way that Jesus can be pictured or portrayed. This is not just a white issue, since you can also find those who would argue from an Afrocentric position that Jesus was definitely an African. From their standpoint it is impossible for them to think that the brown skin and eyes of the Savior could ever be portrayed by a white man.

Other traditions that can work to hinder reconciliation include service lengths (many white churches risk losing attendees if the service runs over an hour, while many black churches may begin and end later than scheduled), interpretation of missions (many white churches view missions as sending missionaries to foreign lands to preach the gospel, while many black churches view missions as meeting the diverse social needs of their communities as they did during segregation), preaching styles (many white preachers will tend to be more "scholarly" by focusing on historical and textual accuracy, while many black preachers will utilize traditional preaching techniques such as "hooping" to emotionally charge their hearers).

We see these issues and think that they are exceptions to our daily experiences but they are not. We all have personal preferences that are shaped by our traditions, and these preferences are what we usually identify as the basis for our interactions with individuals of another racial group. Regrettably the problem is that we continue to emphasize and glory in our cultural traditions to the denial of our Christian transformation, a transformation that has now made us all one in Christ.

Superiority versus Inferiority

An historical overview of black and white relations in the United States quickly reveals that each group has attempted to identify itself as superior, thereby categorizing the other group as inferior. Whites established the pattern in America as they claimed superiority for themselves as masters to justify the inferior position of blacks as slaves. Racial stereotypes that reinforced the superiority of whites and the inferiority of blacks were created and disseminated throughout society. One of the superior/inferior stereotypes that is still present in Christianity is the belief that allowing black and white children to have close fellowship in church will result in the loss of white daughters to black males.

Blacks also developed stereotypes about whites that positioned blacks as superior and whites as inferior. These stereotypes have been disseminated in society to a lesser extent but are well-known among blacks. For example, some African Americans believe that American slavery is not a unique event because whites have always oppressed other racial groups throughout history. If the tables had been turned, they believe, blacks would never have oppressed whites and allowed slavery in America. Many African Americans also believe that whites have a less dynamic form of Christianity than blacks. God is a God of the oppressed and downtrodden and therefore has special compassion for African Americans because their oppression in America was very similar to Israel's bondage in Egypt. This is why, they conclude, God has more greatly blessed the expression of Christianity in the African American community.

Stereotypes, by their very nature, are exaggerations, based in some cases on a kernel of truth or a few similar observations. As a result, every American today has had his or her knowledge of another racial group tainted by racial stereotypes that have been developed through the centuries and continue to be communicated today.

A primary result of this superior/inferior struggle is that blacks and whites have a lack of appreciation for the unique and distinctive characteristics of the other group's church traditions. Therefore whites devalue the spiritual contributions that the Black Church traditions can make to their knowledge and experience of God. The spirituals and gospel songs of black Christians are overlooked as theologically shallow, although they have risen from practical theology, being deeply rooted in centuries of Christian experience lived in the face of great persecution.

Similarly blacks devalue the spiritual contributions the white church traditions can make. Therefore the hymns and choruses of white Christians are disregarded as dry and impersonal, although often they convey precise and foundational doctrines of the faith that have been passed down through the centuries. The Scriptures teach that our personal value is not heightened by our demeaning others but exists only through our esteeming others better than ourselves (see Phil. 2:3–4).

A Lack of Trust

The animosity and suspicion that exist between blacks and whites are so intense that they have caused a deep mistrust to develop between the two groups. The failure of many white Christians to stand up against slavery and discrimination has caused many blacks to distrust whites with the result that they do not want to partner with whites to accomplish a goal, even a spiritual goal. They fear that whites will take over and will attempt to achieve their own goals and disregard the goals of their black partners in the endeavor. This is often echoed in the comment, "Whites always want to rule." It was the reason behind black denominational leaders advising their members to not be involved in Promise Keepers or the reconciliation of black and white Pentecostal groups. This view can also be seen in the suspicion about whites who attend black churches.

Whites on the other hand express their lack of trust in blacks in a commonly held view that blacks have a chip on their shoulder and will therefore seek to get back at whites for years of slavery. Many think blacks hold them at arm's length, not allowing whites who sincerely wish to have a cross-cultural relationship with them to draw close. There is also the fear that as they draw close to blacks, whites leave themselves open to fickle outbursts of anger or for cries of discrimination when circumstances don't go according to the desires of blacks.

A False Sense of Self-Sufficiency

The hurt and distrust that have developed through the history of black and white interaction have resulted in the misconception that we can live separate lives. We can go our own way with no deleterious effects. Because of past events there are many black and white Christians who weekly forget that Christianity is community based—not a geographical community or a racial community but a global community of all those who have placed their trust in Jesus Christ as their Lord and Savior. But the reality is that both black and white Christians continue to view the ministry of racial reconciliation as a peripheral, or optional, ministry and its time has not yet arrived.

A primary reason that Christianity's power is not able to heal the wounds of racism is that many evangelicals do not understand race and the race problem from a biblical perspective. Therefore it is hard to see the Bible's important insights and instruction on how the wrongs of the past and the resultant animosity and separation can be reconciled. We need to examine what the Bible has to say about race and the Bible's instructions on how we are to deal with hostility between people. For if this power is not unleashed to transform society, the fact that the most segregated time of the week is eleven o'clock Sunday morning will continue to be a correct characterization of Christianity in America.

PART 2

THE INTENDED BIBLICAL PATTERN

God has a purpose for his church in respect to racial reconciliation. To discover that purpose, we must obtain a biblical perspective on race by accurately examining and applying what the Bible says. As we study the Bible, we see that the issue there is not racial divisions, as we define race, but ethnic divisions.

Christians must come to realize that racial reconciliation is not peripheral to the ministry of spiritual reconciliation but is rather a natural and inseparable dynamic of it. As we look at the life and ministry of Christ, we see the importance he placed on racial and ethnic reconciliation. This has much to do with the basic nature of his church and is evident in the prominence given to settling divisive ethnic issues in the New Testament church. Understanding this will prepare us to look at our own responsibility to the ministry of racial reconciliation.

RACE IN THE BIBLE

One day a group of blind men encountered an elephant for the first time. These men were not blind from birth and had some idea of the world they could no longer see, but this animal was unfamiliar to them. In an attempt to understand what this animal was like, they began to touch the animal, each touching a different part. One felt the long trunk of the elephant and thought this animal was just a powerful snake. Another felt a tusk and thought that the animal was just a tall rhinoceros. The third man felt a leg of the elephant and thought it was like a tree. In the end they each interpreted the elephant from an experience they had had with other animals or things that seemed to match what they discovered about the elephant. In the end they were all wrong in their attempt to understand what the elephant was really like.

So it is for us if we come to the Bible with a preconceived idea about race and then try to find understanding within its pages. To approach the Bible with this mind-set can cause us to erroneously equate our concept of race with what is revealed in Scripture.

To accurately examine what the Bible says about racial reconciliation, we must begin with the realization that the biblical issue is not racial divisions, as we in contemporary America define race, but ethnic divisions. The Greek word translated *race (genos)* in the New Testament is used to denote a person's descendants (Acts 4:6), a person's family (Acts 7:13), and peoples or nationalities (Mark 7:26). Therefore, the word *race* in the Bible may refer to the origin, lineage, or unity of humanity in that all people are members of the human race (Acts 17:28–29). This common membership means that all people find their origin and source of life in God, they all come from the same original parents (Adam and Eve—Acts 17:26), they are all contaminated by the same disease (sin—Rom. 3:23) that ultimately results in death (Rom. 5:12), and they all have the same need (a relationship with Jesus Christ that can remove the penalties of sin—Rom. 6:23).

Our modern American understanding of race is very different from this. Today we understand *race* to refer to physical, mental, and emotional characteristics that are based on visible physical features (that include but are not limited to skin color, width of nose and lips, and hair type). Individuals and groups who possess certain physical features are expected to act a certain way, and are, therefore, treated in accordance with those expectations. So, for example, whites are expected to have certain physical traits, such as thin lips and a narrow nose. When a person's looks don't match that expectation then he or she may be treated as if he or she is not white but of another racial group. On the basis of such an expectation Babe Ruth was called "Niggerlips" while growing up because of his broad nose and lips, which were considered to be African American–like facial features.[1]

Also the criteria for determining the race of individuals can be inconsistent since the American concept of race tends to be based on personal or social decisions rather than on biological standards. For example, many light-skinned blacks have been able to move into white American society because their physical features were not considered African American. One of the most revealing examples of the imprecision of race measures is the story of Susie Guillory Phipps. In the 1980s Susie Guillory Phipps, the wife of a white business-man in Louisiana, went to court to try to get the racial designation on her birth certificate in Louisiana changed from "colored" to "white." A 1970 Louisiana "blood" law required that persons with one thirty-second or more "Negro blood" (ancestry) were to be designated as colored on birth records; before 1970 "any traceable amount" of African ancestry had been used to define a person as colored. The white-skinned Phipps was the descendant of an eighteenth-century white plantation owner and an African American slave, and that small amount of African ancestry was enough to classify her as "colored." She lost her case against the state.[2] It is important to note that having one black ancestor made this person black, regardless of her external features. But having a white ancestor has never allowed a person with black features to be categorized as a white person in our society.

The Bible's Criterion

The Bible focuses on ethnic divisions and not race. The Greek word *ethnos* is the most comprehensive and most frequently used word to signify people who are grouped together because of a common country or history ("nations" in Matt. 28:19; "nation" in John 11:48). Ethnic distinctions are general characteristics that include a person's nation of origin, language, lineage, customs, and outward features, such as skin color. When familiar racial identifiers, such as skin color, are used in the Bible, it is to distinguish and differentiate between people and people groups (Simeon was called Niger, which denotes his dark complexion, in Acts 13:1).

This attempt to distinguish between people is a normal and acceptable approach we as humans utilize to understand the world around us. My two oldest sons, who were five and four at the time, taught me this truth. One day I mentioned to them that we were going to be having some friends over to our house. They could not picture in their minds the people I was referring to when I said our friends' names. Almost in unison they then said, "Do they have a black face or a white face?" I was stunned. *Where did that come from?* I wondered. Carolyn, my wife, and I had never referred to our friends in terms of color. How could I, a person who was teaching on race relations in various academic and religious settings, fail so greatly in raising my own boys! At this point I did what any other well-adjusted male would do. I blamed their mother.

Just joking. At that point I realized that what my boys had done was to use skin color as one way of distinguishing between the different friends that their parents had. When they were unable to remember the names of family friends, they moved to another level of distinguishing characteristics, which in this case was color. This use of color would have been wrong if my sons had attached different meanings or values to our friends based on the color of their faces. If black faces were always smarter or "good" in contrast to white faces, or vice versa, then my greatest fears would have been realized, for my sons would then be racists. But that was not the case. The differentiation was simply one more aid in distinguishing between what must have seemed to them an overwhelming number of people.

The Bible does not present racial identifiers as indicators of the possession or lack of possession of innate abilities and qualities. The basis for certain people groups being characterized negatively in the Bible is their failure to be obedient to the teachings of Yahweh, the only true God. In the Old Testament this rejection of God is expressed in the opposition of these groups to the people of God, Israel, who were called to model and proclaim God's truths to all people (Gen. 12:1–2; 18:18). When these people groups failed to acknowledge and serve the only true God and to honor his people,

the Bible was then very clear in denouncing them and prohibiting Israel from having intimate relationships with them
(Ezra 9:1–2; Zeph. 2:8–11).

In the New Testament the instruction is the same as the
Bible continues to challenge the people of God, who are now
made up of members from all people groups, to be separate
from those who reject the Word and will of God. So the Bible
calls believers to be a light to all people without allowing the
sinful lifestyles of these people to influence them (2 Cor.
6:14–17; 1 Peter 2:7–12).

Overall, the Bible condemns such groups as the Canaanites, Philistines, Samaritans, and Gentiles (a comprehensive
category identifying all those who are not a part of God's
people) not on the basis of their nationality, but because they
are deficient in their relationship with the true and living
God. Their ungodly lifestyles are the clear manifestations of
their not having such a relationship. Yet the negative characterization of these groups is removed when they accept
God's teachings and walk in his Word. One of the best examples of such a change is found in the Book of Jonah. Most of
us remember Jonah as the prophet who chose to belly dance
with a fish rather than do God's will. But we must also realize that the reason for Jonah's time in the fish was his failure
to deal with his heart problem—his love for others was prejudiced. The book shows how the prophet Jonah, who rep-
resents the rest of the nation of Israel, failed to grasp the universal compassion and love God has for all people.

Jonah's Heart Problem

The story begins with God commanding Jonah to go and
warn the city of Nineveh to repent or be destroyed in forty
days. By running in the opposite direction, Jonah shows that
he would rather see the nation destroyed. Jonah knows that
Nineveh is the capital of the superpower nation Assyria, and
that Assyria would someday ravage Israel. This possibility is

too much to make pro-Israel Jonah want to play a role in bringing Yahweh, Israel's God and protector, into an intimate relationship with Assyria, Israel's greatest national threat. But God teaches Jonah that not only are his arms too short to box with God but that his legs are too tiny to run from God. So Jonah has a change of heart and preaches to Nineveh and a great revival occurs that brings the whole city to repent and submit to God's will. Unfortunately Jonah did not leave his prejudice in the great fish and as the book ends, he angrily stomps off and pouts, hoping that God will change his mind and destroy Nineveh.

God once again deals with his prophet and even orchestrates a few events to teach Jonah the error of his ways. God allows a gourd to grow and the vine provides Jonah comfort. Jonah becomes so attached to the gourd that the Bible states he becomes "very happy" over the gourd. Remarkably this is the only time in the book that this emotion is used in reference to Jonah. God then destroys the gourd, to which Jonah responds with more anger, setting the stage for Yahweh's final words and the end of the book. In Jonah 4:10 God points out to Jonah that he had compassion for a gourd for which he did nothing to make it grow as it blossomed and grew overnight then perished the following morning. Jonah had not cultivated a long-term relationship with the gourd. Obviously Jonah's compassion was selfish and counter to the universal compassion God has for all people. This is driven home in God's final words, which I have paraphrased:

> Am I wrong, Jonah, for sparing the great city of Nineveh in which there are 120,000 people along with many animals? I have labored over them and have supplied all that they have needed to exist and grow. As I appointed the vine, I also appointed the city. Yet you became ecstatic for a plant rather than for a city of thousands that repented and turned to me. You hold the wrong object in esteem! Yes they deserve my punishment, but they can't even distinguish good from wrong

according to my law. When it comes to spiritual matters they can't tell their left hand from their right hand. But you still don't care! (v. 11)

Clearly Jonah was eager to go and prophesy God's blessing on Israel in the time of King Jeroboam II (2 Kings 14:25 is the only other time Jonah is mentioned in the Old Testament), but a revival in Assyria was not what *he* viewed to be in the best interest of the only people God should be interested in—Israel. Jonah did not realize the universality of Yahweh's purpose and compassion. Jonah did not realize that the basis of a relationship with Yahweh is obedience to his will, which goes beyond all ethnic distinctions.

Relationships among God's People

We err, then, when we go to the Bible and equate its references to physical characteristics with the way we in modern America think of race. Approaching the Bible in this way would be similar to believing that the Bible talks about automobiles because Ezekiel saw four "wheels" and "rims" in his vision. Such an interpretative approach has produced much error concerning the biblical message. For example, support for the oppression and segregation of blacks was based on the erroneous teaching that Noah cursed his son Ham, whose name is derived from the Hebrew word denoting "heat or hot" and has therefore been identified as the individual from whom blacks descended, inheriting the curse. A more accurate study, even reading, of the Genesis 9 account shows that it was Canaan (v. 25) who was cursed and not Ham. Furthermore, the focus of the passage is not to show how the various races began but to give the reason why Canaan, and his descendants the Canaanites, were cursed.

An unbiased examination of Scripture shows that various nationalities are mentioned throughout the Bible and that they are even mentioned as being a part of God's people.

Yes, many intermarried into the nation of Israel. Over the history of this country many Christians have argued that God looks down on interracial marriages based on the Old Testament prohibition against Israelites marrying outside of the nation (Deut. 7:1–4; Ezra 9:10–15; Neh. 13:23–27). But those who make this argument fail to note that this prohibition is not given because the people of Israel are superior but to keep God's people from marrying those who could cause them to worship a god other than Yahweh. One of the purposes of marriage for Israelites was to communicate the responsibilities of their covenant relationship with Yahweh so that future generations would continue to preserve and honor that covenant relationship. A marriage to a person who worshiped another god jeopardized the covenant relationship since the Israelite spouse could begin to worship his or her spouse's god or could cause the children of that union to worship that false deity (Exod. 34:14–16).

Contrary to those who would argue that God prohibited interracial and interethnic marriages are the numerous biblical examples of such marriages when religious apostasy was not a concern. For example, Moses married the Cushite—African—woman (Num. 12:1, 9–11). Rahab, the harlot of the Canaanite city Jericho, married into the nation of Israel after she realized that Yahweh is the only true God (Josh. 2:11; Matt. 1:5). There is no indication that Boaz was acting contrary to the will of God when he married Ruth, a woman from Moab (Ruth 4:13–15). Rahab's and Ruth's marriages are important to note since it is through these marriages that the lineages of David and Jesus pass (Matt. 1:5–6, 16).

In the New Testament there is no biblical requirement that Christians marry individuals of the same race. This gives believers the freedom to marry whomever they choose as long as they meet the principal marriage requirement of marrying "in the Lord" (1 Cor. 7:39). The New Testament admonition to not be unequally yoked (2 Cor. 6:14) is in line with the Old Testament prohibition for the people of Israel to not marry foreign women because they were to avoid being led into idolatry.

In summary, it is important for us to note that the God-ordained basis for the ethnic divisions in the Bible is obedience or lack of obedience to God. This is the only criterion for separation that is given in the Bible. All other criteria for divisions within our world are, therefore, illegitimate in the eyes of God. Peter comes to this realization in Acts 10:34–35: "I now realize how true it is that God does not show favoritism but accepts men from every nation who fear him and do what is right" (NIV). As ethnicity in the Bible is not allowed to hide the compassion and purpose God has for all humanity, so racism comes under the same prohibition in our modern society. Such an understanding mandates that the racial divisions within America must not be the standard that Christians use to determine those individuals with whom they should or should not have intimate relationships.

SEVEN

THE MISSING LINK

As we sat waiting for the traffic light's permission to proceed, my son once again asked when I would fix the training wheels on his bicycle. I turned to look at him, saying I would fix them when we got home. Then I added, "But they will be different than what you are used to."

With that I heard a puzzled "huh?"

His raised eyebrows and questioning look told me I'd better explain, so I continued, "I am going to take off one of your training wheels, Norman. Later on I'll take off both of them so that you can ride your bike without training wheels."

His response was as classic and as unexpected as all the other corrective statements his five-year-old lips have uttered. "No, Dad, you're not suppose to ride without training wheels. That's dangerous!"

A few minutes later I thought, that's why racial reconciliation is not a reality in most churches—it's *dangerous.* Racial reconciliation is dangerous to pursue and to maintain. Anytime you bring two groups together who have been divided by years of abuse, oppression, anger, suspicion, and fear and encourage them to love one another, you have a volatile situation, with perhaps an unattainable goal. Similar to my son's acceptance of his training wheels as normal, churches have accepted the present state of race relations as inevitable. For that reason racial unity is viewed as an ideal state that is peripheral to a church's primary task, the proclamation of the gospel. Because this social ministry is viewed as dangerous and peripheral to the spiritual ministry of the gospel, it has not been a priority for many evangelicals. In a class I teach on race relations one of the issues repeatedly raised by seminarians about a church that holds racial reconciliation as a priority is that a focus on this ministry will distract from a proper focus on the gospel. This reservation is unfortunate but expected since the ministry of racial reconciliation is erroneously viewed as detached from the ministry of the gospel.

There is an *integral* link between racial reconciliation and spiritual reconciliation. It is my contention that racial reconciliation should not be viewed as a rival to evangelism and discipleship but as an outgrowth and accentuation of the gospel's ministry. There are three reasons why racial reconciliation, although dangerous, should be seen as linked to God's saving work in Christ and therefore pursued by all committed Christians:

1. Christians must pay attention to the important premise in the Bible that God's actions stand as patterns for the actions of his people.
2. The believer's understanding of reality should be governed by God and not by the culture around him or her.
3. The gospel is evidenced and magnified by the actions of its adherents.

Walk This Way

The first reason that racial reconciliation should be seen as linked to the saving work of God in Christ is the important premise that God's actions stand as patterns for the actions of his people. This is how God mentors his children. Like a parent encouraging his child to follow, the biblical example is clear that God desires his children "to walk this way."

The new command of Jesus in John 13:34 implements this pattern. Jesus teaches his disciples to love one another because he has first loved them. In John 15:12, 16–17 Jesus again commands his disciples to love one another based on his having exemplified that love to them. This pattern is also evident in the justification statements that accompany many of the commands in the New Testament epistles. These letters that were written to the early church sought to give foundational truths and practical instruction based on those truths. For example, we are to forgive one another even as God for Christ's sake forgave us (Eph. 4:32). In respect to marriage the husband's responsibility is based on the pattern of Christ's love for his church (Eph. 5:25–28). Our love for God is based on his first loving us (1 John 4:19). This love God has for us then becomes the standard to which our love for others is to conform (1 John 3:16; 4:19–20).

In respect to the ministry of racial reconciliation God's actions are also a pattern for the actions of his people. God's act of reconciling the races is an outgrowth of his antecedent act of spiritual reconciliation. This is evident in such passages as Colossians 3:10–11 where Paul talks about the nature of the "new self" that is put on at salvation. This new self, because of its union with Jesus that is expressed in the phrase "in Him," is enabled and empowered to fully live the life that God desires from the believer. This is expressed in Paul's description of this new life in Colossians 2:10–14 as "complete" (all that God desires for us to be in ourselves and for him can now be achieved because we are united with Jesus); "circumcised" (the ruling influence of the flesh over the believer's mind, habits, desires, character, and so on has been removed); and "baptism" (the believer is vicariously crucified to this world and is raised with power to live the life that

God desires). On the basis of God's actions expressed in this passage in Colossians 2, the believer is then admonished and given instructions on how to walk in a way that agrees with his or her spiritual reality (Col. 3:1–4:6). Paul's description goes beyond a onetime event as it points to a process that is occurring within the believer. This is noted in the Greek word "renew," which appears only in Colossians 3:10 and in 2 Corinthians 4:16. In both occurrences the word is used to delineate between what existed previously and what is now being created. Also the action of renewal is passive denoting that the process is occurring to the believer. Clearly the Holy Spirit is bringing about this re-creation as we are being made into the "image of the One who created [us]." This new humanity is then described further in Colossians 3:11 as one that has no distinction based on group identification (Greek and Jew), religion (circumcision and uncircumcision), culture (barbarian, Scythian in comparison to the Greeks), or social distinctions (slaves and freemen).[1] The ancient world was full of various barriers that separated people, but Paul highlights these particular ones to show that all barriers are no longer relevant to those who are in Christ. A part of the new self's character is a desire for unity that transcends earthly divisions.[2]

Reconciliation that transcends social divisions is presented in Scripture as God's desire, not in competition with spiritual reconciliation but as a reality that is dependent on a person's first being reconciled to God through Christ. The greatest dividers of humanity (race, gender, class, nationality) are then made inconsequential by the greatest uniter of humanity—Christ. Therefore, as God has used spiritual reconciliation to cancel ethnic and other social divisions, so the church's evangelistic and discipleship ministries must include encouragement, and rebuke if necessary, for new and older Christians to live the racial unity that is a reality in Christ. The necessity of this approach is further validated by the corporate nature of salvation as it places believers into a universal family that is characterized by mutual interdependence and unity.

Michael Green describes this idea of a "redeemed community":

> The Old Testament's hope of the redeemed community is one where God's shalom reigns. The element of personal forgiveness is there, but so is the mutual belonging, the restoration of relationships, the social transformation, the victory over forces of decay and destruction, and God's healing touch. In the New Testament the societal aspect of salvation is strongly stressed, as is its link with healing. To be sure, community and healing will never be complete in this life, any more than salvation will. Their climax lies beyond the grave. But any evangelism that does not make clear God's will to rescue and transform the whole of life, physical and spiritual, and that does not make clear the mutual interdependence of those who are experiencing salvation is deficient. Salvation is a mighty concept. It is God's sovereign act of rescue. It is tasted here and now but only fully enjoyed in the life to come. It touches the whole of life: the notion of merely "saving souls" is profoundly unbiblical. And it embraces individuals in their lostness and fragmentation and puts them into the family of God the Savior that, in turn, is intended to exert a profound effect upon society at large.[3]

From this standpoint the ministry of reconciliation presented by Paul in such passages as 2 Corinthians 5:18 clearly gives the church the responsibility to reconcile men spiritually to God. Yet as we have noted, this ministry should also include our working for the result God has achieved through this spiritual reconciliation, which is unity that transcends racial divisions. The church, therefore, must be about the business of reconciling mankind both spiritually and racially. We must walk as God walks.

Question Reality

The second reason racial reconciliation should be viewed as linked to the saving work of God in Christ is that the believer's understanding of reality must be defined by God and not by the culture around him or her. Yet this is a very difficult goal to attain, for what we see and experience is hard to discount, even if it is erroneous. Why? Because what we see and experience is familiar and is therefore accepted as the norm. As writer Yevgeny Yevtushenko noted, "He who is conceived in a cage yearns for the cage."

By the term *reality* I am referring to the meanings, values, and actions that underlie and shape our lives. *Reality* refers to our social, political, economic, racial, and cultural ideas about ourselves and those with whom we correspond. Our notion of reality is constructed, negotiated, and finally institutionalized to become the basis of our conscious and subconscious interaction with society.[4]

Working in a university town I am familiar with the ubiquitous bumper sticker that beckons its readers to "Question Reality." As a sociologist I realize that the intent of this message is to cause its readers to reexamine what they have been taught about life and society, and what is acceptable and unacceptable. Its appearance on a car usually identifies the car owner as a person who holds a position that is west of the mainstream. Although this bumper sticker was never intended to be a call to a Christian worldview, I believe that it summarizes the point I am making. As the bumper sticker calls for a total reevaluation of the norms in society, because it views these norms as wrong, so the Bible calls the believer to have a different view of the world and its order. It literally calls Christians to question the reality of the world around them and to then accept or reject that reality based on its conformity to the Word of God.

The great challenge for the church to walk counter to the world is that every individual and institution (e.g., family, school, church, government) in our society is molded by this world order in which it exists. Therefore, these institutions will shape the people under their influence by shaping their beliefs and values. In so doing, these institutions work to perpetuate accepted social patterns by categorizing other critiques of the world order as theoretical or erroneous.

The call to see reality from God's perspective is prevalent throughout Scripture. In the Old Testament pervasive idol worship stood as one of the greatest challenges for the nation of Israel to view reality from God's perspective rather than from that of the world around them. For this reason the Old Testament has numerous references to the reality of the only true God who is unlike created idols (Exod. 20:4–5; Lev. 19:4; Deut. 13:6–18; Ps. 96:4; Isa. 44:9–20; Jer. 10:1–16; just to list a few).

In the New Testament a clear contrast is made between the present order of this sinful world, and the reality that is presented by God (1 John 2:15–16). Stephen Mott explains, "The cosmos [world order] we are to hate is human values and conduct insofar as they are organized in opposition to God. Evil is the very fabric of our social existence."[5] The believer is repeatedly called to walk counter to a reality in this world that is constructed by the enemies of the will of God (Eph. 2:1–3; 5:8–12; 2 Cor. 10:3–6). Failure to walk in such a fashion is a failure to see the world as it really is and then we cannot be used to reveal divine reality to a deceived world: "And do not be conformed to this world, but be transformed by the renewing of your mind, that you may prove what the will of God is, that which is good and acceptable and perfect" (Rom. 12:2; see also Matt. 5:13–16; 6:22–24; 1 John 1:5–7).

When it comes to race, the American evangelical church has for the most part been unsuccessful in rejecting the beliefs and values of the world. I believe that the reason for this difficulty is that we have accepted society's norm rather than what God has said is real. Who in their right mind would attempt to accomplish that which is seemingly unattainable and unrealistic? In God's reality, though, racial reconciliation is attainable because Christ has already removed all barriers except one—our choices. Jesus has already made racial reconciliation, as he has our spiritual unity, a positional reality. We are one in Christ regardless of our racial category. Christians are now responsible to make racial reconciliation and unity our experiential reality.

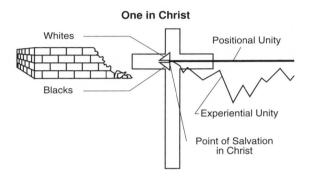

The wall of racism that has separated whites from blacks in American society, like the wall of the law that separated Jews and Gentiles (Eph. 2:14), has been broken down for those who are in Christ. Whites and blacks, regardless of their position in society, in Christ meet at the same point of salvation and continue on from that point unified *positionally* in Christ. Although united as the church, blacks and whites are responsible for *experiencing* that unity in their day-to-day interactions. Unfortunately throughout American history the experiential unity that blacks and whites should have as the church has not equaled the positional unity they have in Christ.[6]

From this standpoint the church's true reality is that the ministry of racial reconciliation and the saving work of Christ are linked. The reality that is evident in Christ, then, must be the reality we seek to achieve.

Faith on Steroids

The ministry of racial reconciliation should be linked to the gospel because the behavior of Christians is evidence of and magnifies the truth of the gospel. The importance of the believer's works to the power of the gospel was made very clear to me during a lunch meeting I had with a Muslim gentleman. After he explained to me the works-based foundation of Islam, I explained that the gospel teaches that faith in what Jesus did on the cross was the Christian's basis for eternal life. He immediately burst into laughter and said, "You guys have it easy!" I responded by telling him that such faith did not excuse Christians from living lives that are pleasing to God. Seeing that he was still enjoying his chuckle, I then pointed to some of my actions, that he was aware of, as proof that I did not take my faith for granted and was living to evidence that faith daily. Only then did he seem to regain his composure and we continued our conversation and meal.

The importance of works to manifest the reality of the gospel is clearly noted in the Bible. The Book of James teaches how important works are to faith. This great letter to Christian exiles gives practical instruction on how the believer is to live. In 2:14–26 James discusses the relationship that behavior has to faith. To understand why James discusses this relationship at this point in the letter, we must note what precedes it. In the previous verses (1–13) James addresses the Christian's standards for viewing people he or she encounters. In verse 1 James straightway deals with the issue by telling the readers to not be partial or show favoritism. The Greek word that is translated "favoritism" literally means "take face." A more contemporary translation is that we are not to take others at face value or treat them based on their outward appearance. Rather we are supposed to see them as God sees them. To judge on the basis of outward appearance reveals personal ignorance (vv. 2–4), social ignorance (vv. 5–8), and spiritual ignorance (vv. 9–13). These verses conclude with an emphasis that is built on James 2:10: *"No command of God can be trivialized, but all must be obediently followed"* (author's paraphrase).

On this note James begins in verse 14 to argue that a faith that does not have evidence is valueless. He states that if a person says that he or she has faith, but it does not manifest itself in works, that faith is of no value. He even goes as far as stating that this faith cannot save a person! This is a very strong assertion that James justifies by using an illustration that presents "a supposition bordering on the ludicrous."[7] The beauty of this illustration is that it pulls us into a situation in which we must make a choice. As we make that choice, our faith is then evaluated. The illustration is of a person who desperately needs clothing and food to make it through the day. If our response consists of mere words, desiring to speak compassion to that person ("Go in peace, be warmed and be filled"), but not an act of compassion toward the individual, James has a low evaluation of *that* faith. If our faith is not enough to move us to save someone from a life of agony on earth, how can it save us from a life of agony in eternity (vv. 24–26)?

James sums up his evaluation of this faith in verse 17 by calling this type of faith *dead*. The reason for this is that faith lives through our lives, through our works. Without the action that comes through our life, faith is lifeless and has no impact on the world of the living. Clearly, then, social action is the incarnation of the gospel. To have faith without works is biblically illegitimate (vv. 20–24). If our faith does not move us to act even when we do not feel like it, our faith is dead. If our faith isn't loving and compassionately reaching out to meet the needs of others, it does no one, not even ourselves, any good (v. 26). But a faith that is manifested in works is a faith empowered to magnify the gospel so that it will reveal Jesus to a lost world (Matt. 5:13–16; 1 John 4:20).

A great example of the effect such evidenced faith can have for the gospel is the story of the mission to the Auca Indians. On January 8, 1956, five young missionaries, one of whom was Jim Elliot, were killed on a river beach in Ecuador. These men died at the hands of the Auca Indians, the very people the missionaries were trying to reach with the gospel. Later a sister of one of the slain missionaries, Rachel Saint, went to live with the Auca Indians along with a young woman, Dayuma, who had earlier run away from the tribe. Rachel Saint later stated:

> You see, for us to be willing to live with them cut straight across the pattern of revenge. They killed our men. Dayuma's brother had killed my brother. Yet we were asking to live with them instead of taking our revenge. Then one day they found that our men had had guns with them when they were attacked and that they could have defended their lives. But they chose to die rather than shoot the Indians. Nothing less than this kind of commitment would have broken the Auca's cultural mindset.[8]

In respect to racial reconciliation this is the type of gospel the world is longing to see. It has for too long *heard* about the love of Jesus without seeing it through love shown between black and white Christians. It has for too long *heard* about the oneness of those in Christ without seeing this unity manifested in day-to-day interactions between the races. Only a gospel that is hoisted high on the back of a living, vibrant, socially manifested faith will greatly impact our humanistic culture for Jesus.

Lesslie Newbigin notes the important impact that the community in which such faith abounds has on society:

> How is it possible that the gospel should be credible, that people should come to believe that the power which has the last word in human affairs is represented by a man hanging on a cross? I am suggesting that the only answer, the only hermeneutic of the gospel, is a congregation of men and women who believe it and live by it. I am, of course, not denying the importance of the many activities by which we seek to challenge public life with the gospel—evangelistic campaigns, distribution of Bibles and Christian literature,

conferences, and even books such as this one. But I am saying that these are all secondary, and that they have the power to accomplish their purpose only as they are rooted in and lead back to a believing community.[9]

Yes, it will take this kind of "steroid-empowered" faith to make a difference in our world. For only this kind of faith in the life of white evangelicals will move them beyond their disinclination—because of the modernist/fundamentalist debates—to bother with social issues and be advocates for African American progress. Only this kind of faith will move black evangelicals to stand boldly against the militant voices of their community to partner with their white brothers and sisters in Christ to achieve unity. This type of faith, which is evidenced through our actions, will magnify the gospel to such an extent that it will challenge the beliefs of our divided society.

It seems apparent that reconciliation, both spiritual and racial, is an integral part of the gospel. Racial reconciliation is not a rival to the gospel; rather it is a result of God's saving work through Christ Jesus. Therefore it is inaccurate to think that we must focus on either the gospel or racial reconciliation as if they were in competition. They cannot be separated, for the gospel *is* reconciliation. Christ himself is our example. His life and that of his early church manifest the gospel of reconciliation.

EIGHT

THE PROOFS
IN THE PATTERN

One of the requests I often received while teaching a seminary class on race relations was for passages and insights that could be used to show church members the importance of racial reconciliation. I was able to direct my students to various New Testament passages that teach the centrality of racial reconciliation to the church's mission, message, mark, and measure of success. As we examine the life and ministry of Jesus, who is clearly presented in the New Testament as the personification, means, and primary advocate of spiritual and racial reconciliation, the New Testament teachings become clear.

The Life of Jesus

The very life of Jesus is one that exudes reconciliation. The coming of the Second Person of the Trinity in human form to die, and by so doing bring us back into an intimate relationship with God the Father, is at the very heart of the biblical concept of reconciliation. As Athanasius noted, "incarnation is reconciliation."[1] Therefore an examination of the Gospels reveals that Jesus' life and ministry intently focused on ethnic inclusion for the purpose of reconciling all people to God.

Jesus' Birth

One of the first indications of Jesus' intended work is the fact that Gentile women are included in his genealogy that is presented in Matthew's Gospel. The highlighting of Ruth the Moabitess and Rahab the Canaanite was a clear emphasis on the significance of Gentiles to the unique personhood of Jesus (Matt. 1:5). Although his heritage was royal through the blood of the great Jewish king David, it was also universal through the blood of these women from two different ethnic groups. Jesus' purpose is also magnified in the wise men who were brought to worship the baby Messiah through an astronomical birth announcement. These men received a special invitation because their presence would communicate the intent and purpose of God to call all nations into an intimate relationship with himself through the coming of Jesus.

A clear pronouncement of this purpose was given in the words of the godly Simeon who, on seeing the baby Jesus, blesses God the Father for this special child who is the very embodiment of God's salvation (Luke 2:30). But Simeon announces another important role of this child in stating that Jesus will be God's instrument of reconciliation in that he will draw *all* people to God. This is evident in Simeon's statements that Jesus is prepared "in the presence of all peoples" (v. 31) because he will be "a light of revelation to the Gentiles" (v. 32). Furthermore, the strong similarity of Simeon's words to Isaiah 52:10 on this occasion is a clear indication that the arrival of Jesus was the prophesied tour de force God had promised to show his greatness on the earth. The power of God is revealed ("bared His holy arm") in the presence of all people ("in the sight of all the nations, that all the ends of the earth may see") to manifest his salvation through Jesus ("the salvation of our God").

Jesus' Ministry

In the three years of Jesus' public ministry, we have numerous accounts of his manifest intention to minister to individuals who were outside of his own ethnic group. As we move through the Gospels we are presented with a Jesus who responds to the request of a Roman centurion who desires him to heal his cherished slave (Luke 7:1–10). We see him reaching out and across ethnic boundaries to heal a woman whom Matthew recognizes as a Canaanite, a group that were bitter enemies of the Jews (Matt. 15:21–28). In Mark 5:1–20 we see Jesus traveling into a gentile region (highlighted by the fact that they raised pigs, animals that were viewed as unclean by Jews) to heal just one person, a demon-possessed man.

A key account in the ministry of Jesus that reveals his high esteem for racial reconciliation is his encounter with the woman at the well in Samaria (John 4:7–45). This was not a chance encounter, as verse 4 states that Jesus "had to" go into Samaria. In other words, Jesus' daily planner listed an appointment that God the Father wanted him to keep. For this reason Jesus went against the religious and social taboos of his ethnic group to save a group of people with whom he was not supposed to associate.

These examples show us that Jesus was a minister of racial or ethnic reconciliation and was not satisfied in ministering only to those of his own ethnic group. Therefore Jesus continually reached out to those who were not like him to model intentional reconciliation through his actions and teachings.

Jesus' Stories

Jesus' teaching ministry, especially the heroes of his stories, revealed his divine view of the world. There is no better example of this than the story of the "good Samaritan" (Luke 10:30–37). For a Jewish rabbi to tell a story in which the hero is a Samaritan is akin to an African American having a white supremacist as his or her story's hero, or a pro-life person having a pro-choice person as his or her story's hero, or a Nazi party member having a Jewish hero in the story, or any other scenario in which an opponent, or enemy, is given the role of hero. These are hard to imagine, aren't they? This is the impact that the story of the good Samaritan had on all those who heard Jesus tell it. Jesus' use of a Samaritan as his story's hero was a clear statement that he would not be hindered by the prejudices of his own racial group who could not see that God's purpose was to bring *all* people together before his throne.

The life and ministry of Jesus thereby show us that reconciliation was at the heart of his purpose. As the Head of the church, Jesus established reconciliation as a characteristic that his followers would manifest as evidence of their relationship with him (John 17:20–23). The New Testament shows that reconciliation is at the heart of the New Testament church's ministry.

The Church

The old saying that the apple doesn't fall far from the tree is very appropriate for our examination of reconciliation in the church's purpose. For as reconciliation, both spiritual and racial, was an integral aspect of Jesus' purpose on earth, we also find it to be an integral aspect of the church's purpose. As we read the New Testament's accounts of the early church, we are given glimpses of the various struggles the church encountered in its endeavor to achieve spiritual and racial reconciliation. As we examine this topic, let us give special attention to the approaches that are used by the first-century church to counter the social order in which it existed, and to the role of the Holy Spirit who now becomes the agent of reconciliation in the church age. Clearly whenever the unity of the church was threatened by questions of a cultural, personal, or doctrinal nature, it was the Holy Spirit who was identified as working to bring the different groups together. To highlight the centrality of racial reconciliation to the church's purpose we will use the lens of the church's mission, message, mark, and measure of success.

The Church's Mission

The mission of the church is given in Matthew 28:19–20 and Luke 24:47, and the church's mission strategy is outlined by the risen Jesus in Acts 1:8. Both the church's mission and mission strategy make clear that from its inception the church was to have a global commitment to bring all people into a personal relationship with Jesus Christ. Yet this great goal was not fully understood or initially pursued as is seen in the inability of a key apostle, Peter, to grasp the universally unifying nature of the gospel.

In Acts 10:9–16 we are given the account of Peter's challenge from God to put aside the cultural prejudice of his people in order to be used by God to accomplish the church's mission. Realizing that Peter's prejudice had been formed through Peter's religious tradition, God reminded Peter that God is the only legitimate basis for any religious tradition. The divine encounter occurs at the end of one of Peter's times in prayer. Peter becomes hungry, and while food is being prepared for him, he falls into a trance. In this trance he sees a sheet, or maybe a tablecloth in this context, lowered from heaven containing all sorts of animals. A hungry person seeing these animals might have desired to make a meal out of them, but not Peter. He had no such desire because as a Jew, he considered all the animals on the menu unacceptable, according to the dietary standards set for the Jews by God.

God told Peter to "kill and eat!" thereby showing that the ancient standards were no longer to hinder Peter from partaking of animals formerly forbidden. Yet Peter continues to hold to his standards by responding "No way, Lord, I have never eaten these things before and I won't start now" (my translation). I hope you have caught the great incongruity of Peter's response to his God. Here is a servant of the living God, who calls him "Lord," responding to a command from his Master by saying in essence, "I will absolutely not yield to your will."

When God responds, "What God has cleansed, no longer consider unholy" (v. 15), he is reminding Peter that he is in charge and that he is the One who established the standards Peter is now clinging to so tightly. God communicated that what he has now made acceptable and right, Peter should no longer consider unacceptable. But Peter does not budge from his position even though the command is given two more times. Peter's refusal to change shows how deeply the dietary standards of Peter's Jewish culture were ingrained in him. These standards were so entrenched in Peter's mind that even the God who initially established them could not rescind them in three attempts. Finally, the sheet and animals are taken back into the sky untouched.

While Peter contemplates the significance to his life and actions of this vision, God provides an opportunity for him to act on the vision for the benefit of the church's mission. The opportunity is presented in the form of messengers from a Gentile centurion requesting Peter's presence. The Holy Spirit connects the vision with the Gentile messengers' arrival by commanding Peter to go with these individuals with whom he would not normally have associated. In a statement that is very reminiscent of God's earlier command for Peter to eat the animals because God cleansed them (v. 15), he now says, "I have sent them Myself" (v. 20).

Arriving at Cornelius's house, Peter then makes a statement (vv. 34–43) that reveals his new understanding of the significance of the vision to his ministry and to the mission of the church. Peter's realization is manifested in his statement in verse 34 that the church is to be a reflection of God's character in that it cannot show partiality. Because God does not show partiality, neither should his church. For that reason the person who believes in Jesus, despite his or her race or nationality, is fully accepted by God (vv. 35, 43). The great proof of that acceptance was the Holy Spirit's falling on the Gentile believers who were present (11:15–18).

Clearly the nature and mission of the church is different than what the Jews had come to accept as God's modus operandi. The church is to have a universal mission that brings all people into a reconciling relationship with God and with one another (Acts 11:1–18; Eph. 2:1–22). As Peter learned, and later taught other Jewish church leaders in Jerusalem, ethnic diversity is an integral attribute of the church's mission.

The Church's Message

The message of the church is an impartial invitation to everyone. All who trust in Jesus will gain eternal life. This invitation was first extended by Jesus (see John 6:37–40), and the church has since been given the responsibility to communicate this invitation to all people (Matt. 24:14; Mark 13:10). But as we have seen in Acts 10, the "everyone" of this great invitation became a major issue for the church as it struggled to accept its universal proclamation. Still, the message of spiritual and racial reconciliation continued as a major dimension of the church's glorious proclamation to the world.

The message of the church appears throughout the New Testament, but one of its most eloquent messengers was Paul. On one great occasion when Paul was moved to address the superstitious idol worship of the learned Athenians, he called them to place their trust in Jesus Christ based on the creatures' responsibility to their creator (Acts 17:24–29). Although in times past that responsibility may not have been clearly realized, as is evidenced in the Athenians' altar "To An Unknown God," Paul proclaims to them that this true God has now made it perfectly clear how *everyone* can enter into an intimate relationship with him. In this setting a key point that Paul does not fail to communicate is that Jesus Christ has come to reconcile all of humanity to God. And Paul expresses that nonnegotiable is the fact that Jesus was publicly proven to be God's intermediary by God's raising him from the dead. When Paul speaks of Jesus' resurrection, the Athenians quickly lose interest because the concept of a bodily resurrection does not match their view of reality and the world. Despite the result, Paul was unwavering in proclaiming the essentials of the gospel to be faithful to the church's message.

Paul's message in Athens was not the only time that Paul was unwavering in his presentation of the whole gospel even when he knew that a failure to accommodate the prejudiced worldview of his hearers might cost him his audience. Another interesting account is presented in Acts 21–22 where, in this case, a failure to compromise almost cost Paul his life.[2] The account begins with Paul's attending the temple and, because of his previous proclamations and ministry supporting racial reconciliation, he is suspected of taking a Gentile into the Jewish temple in Jerusalem. On the basis of this guilt by association, a group of Jews stir up the Jewish population in the city to seize and kill Paul. The riot that ensues is so great that soldiers from the Roman garrison run down and prevent Paul from being beaten to death (v. 32). While being taken to the barracks of the Roman soldiers, Paul requests the opportunity to speak to the mob and is given permission to do so. Gaining their attention Paul speaks to this Jewish mob in Hebrew, their own language, presenting them the gospel.

The crowd listens intently throughout Paul's presentation until he touches on an aspect of the gospel that Paul believes is too essential to leave out. This is God's desire for all, even Gentiles, to enter into a personal relationship with him, and it is for the accomplishment of this goal that Paul states that he has been commissioned by God (Acts 22:21). With this announcement the session comes to a stormy and abrupt conclusion (Acts 22:22–24).

The key point that must be made is that the gospel message is far beyond the social, cultural, political, and even religious norms the world holds. We must proclaim the standards that God has set—that *all* people are called to a relationship with God and one another that is uniquely different from what they have ever experienced.

The Church's Mark

As Jesus prayed for all who would believe in him until his return—a group better known as the church—Jesus focused on one mark, or characteristic, that they would need to manifest (John 17:20–23). Although there are many characteristics he could have chosen, the one he focused on was unity because it best reflected a characteristic of God that the world was sure to note, a unity that went beyond the earthly differences that so commonly separated people: "I in them, and Thou in Me, that they may be perfected in unity, that the world may know that Thou didst send Me, and didst love them, even as Thou didst love Me" (v. 23).

Although the church's mission and strategy were clearly laid out to include the importance of drawing all people to Jesus, the challenge of this formidable responsibility was quickly realized by the New Testament church. Even bringing together Jews of different ethnic backgrounds—Palestinian and Hellenistic (Greek)—resulted in a threat to their unity based on concerns about equality and commitment (Acts 6). The Greek Jews believed that the Palestinian Jews, who led the first church, were overlooking their Greek widows. In response the leaders of the church selected men who had a good reputation, were filled with the Holy Spirit, and were wise to deal with the situation. The character of these men was important because it indicated that the Holy Spirit had total control over their lives, and that such individuals would allow the Spirit to use them to achieve peace and unity among God's people in the midst of a potentially disruptive situation. Clearly the early church knew that the Spirit was the one who would enable unity to be achieved and sustained so that the church's overall mission could be accomplished.

The importance of such Holy Spirit–controlled individuals to the church's achieving God's goal of reconciling humanity is evident in the actions of one of those men selected in Acts 6—Philip. In Acts 8:26–40 Philip is taken by the Spirit to join an Ethiopian government official on his journey and to communicate the gospel to him. By his submission to the Spirit, Philip becomes the channel through which the gospel is communicated to the second Gentile convert identified in the Book of Acts (Nicolas in Acts 6:5 seems to be the first), and by which the gospel is communicated to another people group and culture.

Philip's submission to the Holy Spirit and his obedience to the will of the Holy Spirit made him an important agent in the furtherance of the church's mission. These two accounts of the ministry of Philip reveal the great significance of the church's mark of reconciliation and the importance of yielded servants to achieving that goal.

The Church's Measure of Success

The measure of the success of any endeavor is whether the targeted mission is accomplished. Jesus asserted that the mission of the church would be accomplished. All who were to enter into a relationship with the Father through Jesus would indeed obtain that goal (John 6:36–39). After Jesus ascended into heaven, the commission was passed down from the Son to his church. The Book of Revelation declares that the goal will be achieved, revealing that in the end the church will be comprised of all those who have been gathered from all nations of the earth.

And when He had taken the book, the four living creatures and the twenty-four elders fell down before the Lamb, having each one a harp, and golden bowls full of incense, which are the prayers of the saints.

And they sang a new song, saying,

"Worthy art Thou to take the book, and to break its seals; for Thou wast slain, and didst purchase for God with Thy blood men from every tribe and tongue and people and nation.

"And Thou has made them to be a kingdom and priests to our God; and they will reign upon the earth."

Revelation 5:8–10

Clearly the importance of racial reconciliation to the purpose of our Lord and of his church stands as a clear incentive for us to hold this ministry as a priority for our lives and our ministry. Let us now consider how such a ministry can take root and grow.

PART 3

POSSIBILITIES FOR CHANGE

What will this focus on the ministry of reconciliation look like in the lives of churches and Christians? Every church in America today is communicating some message about the relevance of salvation in Jesus Christ to the racial situation in our country and about God's ability to heal the divisions separating humanity. There are five models of reconciliation that operate in churches and Christian organizations today. They span the continuum from segregation to real unity in Christ.

Being agents of reconciliation is a responsibility that every Christian leader and layperson must take seriously. As we focus on our responsibility, we can develop the personal characteristics and strategies that will encourage our fellow believers to come together as one reconciled and united body in Christ.

NINE

THE RECONCILIATION CONTINUUM

As Christ's body, it is the continuation of the incarnation; it is the agent of Christ for reconciliation.
Stephen Charles Mott

One of the principles my parents repeatedly emphasized during my childhood was, "Your actions will communicate either positive or negative information about our family and your upbringing. Make sure it's positive." This has been one of the many motivations for my attempt to live a commendable and upright life. The simple fact that what I do has a bearing on how my parents' ability to raise a child is evaluated is a profound motivator. Similarly, every Christian, church, and Christian organization today must realize that they are communicating some message about God's ability to mold their lives. More specifically, each Christian communicates a great deal about the relevance of salvation in Jesus Christ to racial reconciliation and whether God has endowed his children with any special gift that can heal the racial divisions separating people.

Such a realization should lead us to first understand the reconciliation models that are being used today and then to adopt a model that best reflects God's plan for the reconciliation of the races. The reconciliation continuum below shows the range of models in use today. It consists of five types of churches or models of reconciliation: segregation; differentiation; assimilation; intentional, but irrational; and what I call "inHIMtegration."

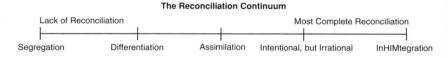

A general characterization of the first two church types is that they are exclusive. The first type, segregation, is not valid in all its manifestations in representing Christ's church and as a model of reconciliation. The validity of the second, differentiation, depends on the intentions of its leaders. The latter three church types are inclusive and are, therefore, closer to the biblical concept of reconciliation.

As we begin to examine these church types, there are two presuppositions that will guide us. First, the oneness of all those who are in Christ is a reality that we must now live in and live out. Second, my intent is not to say that every church must be multiracial. Obviously a logical counterargument to such a position is that there are some geographical areas where the representation of different groups in the general population would make a multiracial church almost impossible. The key issue, though, is that a church and its leaders must be willing to be multiracial if the opportunity arises.

Exclusive Church Types

Segregation

The segregated church does not want individuals to become members or, in extreme cases, to even attend if their race is different from that of the current members. These churches were most evident in the South during the pre-Civil Rights period where blacks were barred from entering whites-only churches. Although not as prominent, this church type also existed in the North. During the 1960s, as white church members observed racial violence and the militancy of some blacks, they instructed their deacons to stand at church doors and bar blacks from entering. For some this was a temporary measure but for others it was a more permanent policy. One example of this is Temple Baptist Church, of Redford, Michigan. Temple Baptist, which had five thousand men, women, and children in its Sunday school classes in 1955, had an unwritten policy of not allowing African Americans into their membership.[1] This policy was changed in 1986.

The Segregation Model

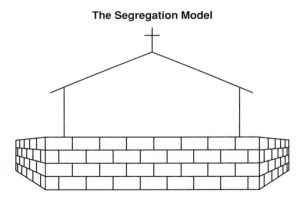

There are various reasons forwarded by these churches to explain their prejudice, but the most fundamental is an erroneous biblical belief that blacks are inferior to whites and should therefore worship separately. If the Nation of Islam were a church, it would fit the segregated church category since their justification for the separation of the races is that it is God-ordained.

Leaders of such churches believe either that one race is inferior to the other or that to challenge the beliefs of their people will hinder church growth. Leaders who are determined to not rock the boat do not want to jeopardize their positions as leaders. Even when they believe racism is wrong, some leaders fear challenging the racist views of their people and risking their position of leadership. Their job or position has become more important than their convictions. The only way change will come to such a church is if those favoring segregation die, leave, or change their minds.

Clearly this church type is biblically invalid but continues to be well represented in North America. An example of the continued existence of this model and the challenge a leader with a differing conviction must face was given to me by a seminary student in one of my classes. The student, whom I will call Tom, shared that during his first year of pastoring a 225-year-old church in North Carolina, he invited an interracial couple—a white male and a black female—to a Sunday worship service. When he had first extended the invitation to the couple, they declined, "knowing full well the bigoted mind-set of some of the members of our church." Tom said he had been aware of the bigotry to a degree but he thought, "Surely the majority of our good Christian folks would have no problem with a black woman just visiting the church to worship." He was wrong!

When the couple and their two children sat down, four people immediately got up and walked out of the building. Tom received a very "threatening" phone call that afternoon, and after the Wednesday Bible study all the deacons called for a special meeting. Tom was given four reasons for their not supporting his invitation to a black woman and her family to attend their church:

1. There was a good "black church" a mile down the road with the same name. Tom's church had helped start this church over one hundred years ago specifically for black people.
2. This was a family church and none of the members

wanted blacks in the church, especially mixed-race couples that would send the wrong message to kids.

3. Blacks were "different" in their ways and in their culture, and mixing them in the church would negatively affect their white culture and traditions.

4. Tom had lied in his initial pastoral interview when he had been asked about bringing blacks into the church. When Tom was asked about his views on integrating the church in his job interview, he stated that he would not seek to integrate blacks into the congregation via membership without following the prescribed order.

Needless to say Tom was forced to resign. In addition to the other astonishing details of this account is the fact that it occurred in 1995!

A similar account is given of Pastor Bruce Edwards of Plains Baptist Church in Plains, Georgia. In 1976 the pastor wanted the church to remove its 1965 policy to "bar Negroes and other civil rights agitators" from services and to remove its longer-standing policy barring blacks from membership. The nation watched as the church narrowly voted against motions supported by all but one deacon to have the pastor resign or be fired. The prominence of the church's vote was based on the church membership of then President-elect Jimmy Carter. President Carter supported the removal of the attendance and membership ban and had stated in opposition to the 1965 ban, "This is not my house or your house. I will never vote to kick anyone out."[2] In the end the church voted to change the policy.

Differentiation

The differentiation church type chooses intentionally to not attract individuals of another racial or ethnic group. This decision comes from a fear that church members will then have to give up the expression of their *racial or cultural unique-*

ness in their church gatherings. This racial or cultural unique-ness may be expressed in the speaking of a non-English language or other cultural distinctives such as dress, food, music, and so on. Examples of such churches can include certain African American churches and many non-English speaking churches, such as Latino, Chinese, or Korean churches.

The Differentiation Model

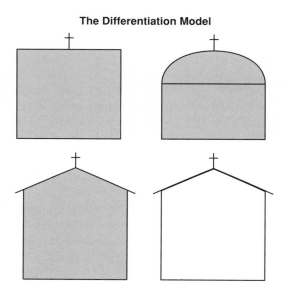

The reason for the existence of these churches is a great appreciation by the group of its culture, history, worship form, and/or language. The fear of church members is that the church will have to accommodate those of another race or culture who might come to visit or join. The leader of such a church realizes the limited audience of the church but sees this as a fair trade-off for honoring the group's distinctiveness. For people and leader there is great concern that if people join from other cultures, especially the majority culture, the church will lose their appreciation and esteem for their founding group's distinctiveness.

I believe that this church is valid if it is hospitable to visitors and members who are different from its intended target group. The greatest danger for such a group, though, is that they will become so proud of their distinctives that they make people uncomfortable who are different from the group or worse, they will view them with contempt. If this occurs, this church type has then fallen into the segregated church model.

Inclusive Church Types

Assimilation

Assimilation is when a church or Christian ministry welcomes and may even put a staff member in place to identify with an incoming racial or ethnic group. Yet in every other aspect, the church or ministry stays the same. No attempt is made to change the musical style or to be sensitive to how the new ethnic group is represented in the Sunday school material. The new group literally becomes a church within a larger church if it decides to keep its distinctiveness. In most cases, though, the incoming group is expected to change in order to "fit in." They must become like the majority, or dominant, group and there are no planned attempts to allow the cultural distinctives of the minority group to influence what is already being done. This church type is the most common model today of those seeking to achieve "racial reconciliation." Prime examples of this approach are mission churches built in Africa and many other countries by European and European American missionaries. The culture of the dominant group, in this case the white missionaries, is seen as the standard to which all converts have to conform to enter the church's membership. Please note that this church type is seen not only in predominantly white churches today but also in predominantly ethnic churches.

This church model is trying to keep from messing around with a good thing. Once a church has attracted a certain group

The Assimilation Model

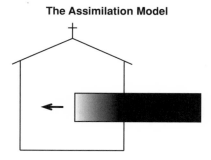

of people, there becomes a unity in similarity that can be challenged through diversity. This challenge is decreased by a diminishing of the degree to which the minority group, in respect to either power or size, causes change. The best means then for limiting minority group influence is to emphasize majority rule and conformity to the majority. Any activity highlighting the characteristics of the minority group is presented as part of a special event or presentation. The leader of such a church is usually happy to see the members of another minority group visit and even join the church, but mistakenly equates the presence of these individuals as evidence that racial reconciliation is being achieved.

A common attempt to achieve greater ethnic representation in a church fits into the assimilation model. The approach is to invite ethnic churches to either share the facility or periodically participate in combined services. The inviting church is attempting to encourage ethnic growth in its congregation by demonstrating its openness to cross-cultural fellowships. The greatest flaw in this attempt is that the inviting church is not always open to sharing ownership and power in the church.[3]

There are two reasons for the prevalence of this model in churches historically and, especially, today. First, this model is the easiest and safest of all the inclusive approaches to reconciliation. The burden for substantial change is on the incoming group rather than on the group that is already present. For that reason this model safeguards what is already the norm and keeps the incoming group from rocking the boat. Minor or cosmetic changes in what both groups have experienced to that point may be made but these changes will not be significant enough to cause concern for the majority group. Second, this model is familiar to most Christians since it mirrors the system of integration that is operating in the world around them. Unfortunately, a church under this model ends up operating as other civil institutions rather than as the divinely initiated institution it is. When mere integration is the focus, the effort is to move diverse racial groups into close social, economic, and political relationships to obtain for minority groups political power and equality. Therefore, *representation* is the measure of success rather than *reconciliation*. In describing this type of integration that is only concerned with removing segregation, Martin Luther King Jr. stated, "It leaves us with a stagnant equality of sameness rather than a constructive equality of oneness."[4]

This attempt to produce equality through close interaction has not, in and of itself, been successful in causing a change in a person's heart condition toward others. Biblical reconciliation on the other hand does not seek to bring people together to give them power and to create equality. Rather, it makes all those in Christ spiritually equal in stature and power with one another, and on this basis demands that they now live out this new reality.

Intentional but Irrational

The intentional but irrational model is a church or Christian ministry that intentionally works to bring members of another group in and also works to have their culture and uniqueness represented throughout the ministry. The attempt is genuine and the aim is to become unified by not allowing the racial and ethnic issues of society to affect their oneness. Even though this model may achieve a great amount of unity and approach the biblical ideal, there is still a major flaw that time and growth will reveal. The flaw is that there is a written or unwritten policy to not differentiate on the basis of race. This approach creates an irrational or artificial environment that only exists when and where the church's members gather. With this policy, the church does not transform the prejudices and thoughts of its members by addressing them openly through truth and love but rather attempts to suppress them for the sake of unity.

An example of this church type was Circle Church of Chicago, Illinois. Circle Church was a multiracial, multicultural church that intentionally sought to manifest biblical reconciliation. Unfortunately race issues were not addressed from black and white perspectives and this led to the dominance of one perspective. This situation later led to a church split along racial lines.[5]

The Intentional but Irrational Model

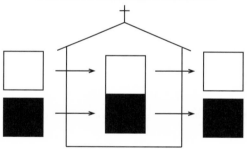

Members of such churches have a strong desire to see individuals of other racial groups be a part of their church and they enjoy the fellowship they have with them. Unfortunately this church's view of unity in Christ means that no one voices discontent or displeasure. Therefore no one raises racial issues or challenges racial views because to do so might be considered contentious. The leader of such a church believes that the issues of the world are secondary to the issues of the

Word. Issues such as racism are seen as the problem of the world system and since believers are no longer vested in that system, especially when gathered as a church, they need not be concerned with it.

This leader erroneously views the church as other-world in mission rather than counter-world in mission. As an other-world community the present world system is overlooked as irrelevant to the life of the believer because it is a temporary state of existence. This can be characterized as a "pie-in-the-sky" approach. In contrast, a counter-world community perspective would demand that the erroneous views of the present world system be openly addressed and countered. This perspective is evidenced in both the corporate gathering of believers and in the individual lives of these believers as they live counter to the system they operate within. (This is discussed further under the inHIMtegration church model.)

The pattern of thought behind this model was highlighted for me at a reconciliation meeting comprised of male and female African Americans, Latinos, and European Americans. A participant protested on the basis of Galatians 3:28—"There is neither Jew nor Greek, there is neither slave nor free man, there is neither male nor female; for you are all one in Christ Jesus"—that the meeting's participants were continuing to divide the body of Christ by using the designation "black church." I was immediately struck by the irony of this evaluation at such a meeting. Reconciliation does not demand that we negate our differences in order to unite. We are setting ourselves up for a fall if we believe that the Galatians 3:28 passage calls us to no longer be what we are. Note that there are still distinctions between us in the body of Christ: women still bear children and men still have a different genetic makeup. The emphasis of this passage, and of biblical reconciliation, is that worldly differences are not to hinder us from fellowshiping together. True fellowship based on reconciliation is fellowship that goes beyond our similarities and glories in the fact that, although we have differences, we are yet *one*. The inability of the intentional but irrational church type to understand Galatians 3:28 in this way hinders its ability to reconcile its members to one another and to impact the world system.

InHIMtegration

When a church makes intentional choices to mix, accept, represent, and manifest racial and ethnic differences, but at the same time magnifies to a greater extent the oneness of believers in Christ, I call it inHIMtegration. I coined the term to describe the creation of Christ, in himself, of a new humanity as seen in Ephesians 2:13–16. This new creation now neutralizes all worldly divisions and becomes the epitome of integration for all those who are in him.

In this model intentional efforts are made to address issues and differences so that they can then be dealt with in healthy ways. Then and only then can the Holy Spirit be free to heal and unify believers into the reality of their oneness. The failure of diversity training or integration is that its aim is to mix the races and hope for an attitude change. InHIMtegration, on the other hand, begins with the premise that believers are already one in Christ and must not live the divisiveness that surrounds them. Therefore believers are to challenge the erroneous beliefs and actions they and their fellow believers have come to accept as reality. As noted black historian John Hope Franklin stated, "You change hearts by changing heads."[6] One of the best examples of this model's implementation is a Promise Keepers conference. At these gatherings an intentional strategy is utilized to bring various races and cultures together in order to have the Word of God address and reconcile the division that has alienated these men. At these conferences such challenging subjects as ownership of and forgiveness for past discrimination are addressed and commitments to live out the oneness in Christ are encouraged.

The InHIMtegration Model

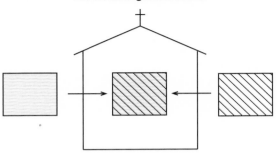

The greatest strength of this approach is that it recognizes that racism is interwoven into every aspect of American society yet works to magnify the spiritual reality of the unity that exists for believers in Christ. Another strength is that this approach allows individuals to express pride in their culture and heritage as an aspect of their identity in Christ.

Biblically we see the inHIMtegration approach to reconciliation espoused in the account of the Jerusalem Council in Acts 15. The context is that many Gentiles have come to the faith under the ministry of Paul and Barnabas (Acts 14:27). Unfortunately certain men of Judea came into the group and began to teach that Gentiles must become Jews to be saved and to enter the church. With the large number of Gentiles becoming Christians, the issue is deemed important enough to send Paul and Barnabas to Jerusalem. There they sit down with the apostles and elders at the premier Christian church of that time. The attitude of the believers in Jerusalem is strongly pro-Jewish, as they are later described in Acts 21:20 as "zealous for the Law." The group considers but rejects the call for Gentiles to become Jews before becoming a part of the church. Instead, the Gentiles are advised to keep their cultural distinctiveness and adhere to certain *"essentials"* for them to be brought into the same church with Jewish Christians. Although these essentials had important ramifications for the Christian walk of Gentiles, they were even more significant for the peaceful coexistence of Jewish and Gentile believers who would now have close interaction in the church (Acts 15:10–11, 28–29).

Of all the options on the reconciliation continuum this church type is the ideal or the best representative of biblical reconciliation. In this church type reconciliation is seen (in the presence of diverse races and cultural expressions), heard (in the style used for music and the presentation of God's Word), and is also felt (in the fellowship of believers through solid actions of love and concern).

The inHIMtegration church model can be achieved through at least four different approaches. An already established church may reach out in an attempt to have other ethnic groups join the church and actively participate. Another approach is for a church to be started with the mission of becoming a multiracial congregation. Or two or more churches that are already ministering to differing ethnic groups may decide to merge to create a multiracial church. A fourth approach is to have one church begin different ethnic congregations within the same facility and under the same church name. Although this last approach has the potential of becoming a "landlord" relationship, it legitimately fits into the inHIMtegration model if there is an intentional strategy to bring these various congregations together to influence the life and structure of the larger church. This approach is a lot harder to achieve, but there are instances in which this format has worked.[7]

Regardless of the avenue for arriving at the inHIMtegration church type, the model that comes closest to the ideal of biblical reconciliation, certain steps must be followed and preparations made for this church type to work. The next two chapters examine the roles of leaders and people in the establishment of such a ministry model.

TEN

THE BUCK STOPS HERE

John Maxwell has repeatedly stated, "Everything rises and falls with leadership." This truism is most important as it relates to the ministry of racial reconciliation. Whether the leader is black or white, overseeing a church or a Christian organization, working in the suburbs or in the inner city, the dangers that line the path of guiding God's people to understand and live out their oneness in Christ are real and challenging. Yet this ideal will not be achieved without godly and dedicated leaders. For this reason this chapter presents six practical insights for leaders who wish to guide their organizations and motivate their people to be active participants in the ministry of biblical reconciliation.

Prepare Your Steps with Prayer

During his five years of pastoring a predominantly white church that was transitioning into a multiracial church, Curtiss DeYoung, now of Twin Cities Urban Reconciliation Network, noted that as he was dealing with racial reconciliation, other reconciliation issues began to emerge, such as the need of believers to repent and forgive past wrongs. From this experience he recommends that any person going into such a ministry must above all else be "prayed up." He would even go as far as recommending that a prayer ministry be established to focus solely on race relations in that ministry. Although leaving the church at the end of five years feeling "whipped," Curtiss DeYoung is still strongly committed to the ministry of racial reconciliation. Many pastors who have worked in this type of ministry echo his outlook on the ministry of racial reconciliation—it is both difficult and worthwhile. Yet the life of Jesus and the early church are clear testimonials that believers can only accomplish the goals God has intended for them to accomplish when they submit to him through prayer. A tour through the life of Jesus is marked by the prominence of prayer.

The Beginning of Jesus' Ministry

Jesus began his ministry with prayer, as Luke 3:21 notes: "Now it came about when all the people were baptized, that Jesus also was baptized, and while He was praying, heaven was opened." Although this is the earliest occasion in which we are told that Jesus prayed, the pattern of prayer he reveals throughout his ministry shows a habit that must have been firmly established in his early life. In response to his baptism and prayer, both acts of obedience and commitment to God, Jesus is empowered and recognized for the ministry that God has prepared him to accomplish.

Jesus' Ministry Priorities

Jesus maintained his ministry priorities through prayer. Another revealing occasion of prayer in our Lord's life is recounted in Mark 1:35–38. After his baptism Jesus travels north to engage in a marathon of ministry activities. In one of the most incredible days of his early ministry, Jesus enters the town of Capernaum and through a string of ministry acts he turns this seaside community and its surrounding communities on their head. First, he enters into the synagogue and teaches a powerful lesson, followed by the exorcism of a demon-possessed man. Then he goes to Simon's house and heals his mother-in-law. As if all that he has done is not enough, the people begin to bring him all those who are ill and demon-possessed. So great is the crowd that Mark says, "the whole city had gathered at the door" (v. 33). Can you imagine the scene as Jesus works late into the night expelling demons and overpowering diseases? Now that is an action hero!

Jesus must have been exhausted from the incredible activities of the previous day; compare Mark 5:30 where we are given some indication that Jesus' healing ministry may have been physically taxing. Yet we see the priority that prayer held in Jesus' life. Very early the next morning—this may have been between 3 and 6 A.M. since it was still dark—Jesus was up and praying in a lonely place. The reason for his need to withdraw and pray was to keep his focus on his purpose. His disciples were now beginning to offer a path of least resistance—seeking the temporary applause of people rather than the more challenging will of God. Jesus' popularity was the focus of his disciples, but Jesus knew that he could not live without an intimate and constant relationship with God. For this reason he prayed, and his prayer continued to move him to a lonely cross to fulfill God's will.

Selecting Leaders

Jesus selected his key leaders through prayer. At an early point in his ministry, Jesus needed to select his apostles. He was so focused on this great responsibility that he became oblivious to time and spent all night in prayer.

And it was at this time that He went off to the mountain to pray, and He spent the whole night in prayer to God. And when day came, He called His disciples to Him; and chose twelve of them, whom He also named as apostles.

Luke 6:12–13

The need for prayer in selecting leaders is affirmed by Pastor Michael Posey of the Church of the Harvest. He notes that one of the greatest difficulties he encounters is being intentional about having multiracial leadership in the church without having quotas or being preferential in preparing and selecting leaders. In his experience he has often found it easier to select whites to key leadership roles because of their greater exposure to formal Bible training and different types of church ministries. Prayer is an important part of the process when diversity in leadership is sought.

While recently reviewing my prayer journal, I noticed that the Lord had laid on my heart the need to pray for future leaders in our church four years before we started the church and seven years before we actually appointed our first elders. In the nine years since that journal installment I have seen the Lord bless our church with godly leaders from diverse racial backgrounds. At the same time I have seen many others who seemed to be capable leaders revealed to be otherwise before they were placed in a leadership position. In each of these circumstances I am sure that my prayers for the Lord to show us the godly leaders he provided has made the difference.

The End of Jesus' Ministry on Earth

Jesus concluded his earthly ministry in prayer. It's interesting that Jesus' betrayer knew exactly where Jesus could be found, because he was in a favorite prayer location during the greatest crisis of his life. The impending cross would remove him from the intimate relationship he had always enjoyed with his heavenly Father. As he faced this inevitability, he prayed, "My Father, if it is possible, let this cup pass from Me; yet not as I will, but as Thou wilt" (Matt. 26:39).

Jesus' Church and Prayer

Jesus' church must pray. In light of Jesus' strong commitment to prayer is it any wonder that Jesus' expectation was that his church would accomplish its ministry on its knees. Jim Cymbala of the Brooklyn Tabernacle identifies our Savior's expectation:

> Have you ever noticed that Jesus launched the Christian church, not while someone was preaching, but while people were praying? In the first two chapters of Acts the disciples were doing nothing but waiting on God. As they were just sitting there . . . worshipping, communing with God, letting God shape them and cleanse their spirits and do those heart operations that only the Holy Spirit can do . . . the church was born. The Holy Spirit was poured out.[1]

Be a Personal Reconciler

A very clear principle of biblical leadership is that a person must give evidence of his qualifications for leadership (he must *be*), before he is given the authority of a leader of others (before he can *do*). This principle is set forth most clearly in the life qualifications that are given for the positions of elders and deacons (1 Tim. 3:1–13; Titus 1:6–9). A man must first evidence his character and leadership traits through his life before he is given the opportunity to act in the role of elder or deacon. There are many reasons for this requirement but a primary one is that commitment breeds commitment, and there is no greater way of showing one's commitment to a cause than to give one's life, a person's most priceless possession, to that cause. On this basis a leader can then challenge others through word and deed to "wholeheartedly follow me to this goal!"

Being Consistent

In respect to race relations, you, as a leader, must live a racially reconciled life. Don't fool yourself into thinking that you can attempt this ministry without first giving your life to it. You may talk about racial reconciliation but it will have no impact until your commitment to this ministry can be seen. You must show your love for members of other racial and ethnic groups if you desire those you lead to do the same. You can lead people only to where you are! As Ralph Waldo Emerson stated, "What you are shouts so loudly in my ears I cannot hear what you say." Be assured that your love for all people will be repeatedly tested and your response to these tests observed by those you are attempting to lead.

The apostle Paul was aware of a leader's need to be consistent in modeling a commitment to the ministry of racial reconciliation. At one point he challenged Peter and even Barnabas as to their failure in this area. He writes about it in Galatians 2:11–14. Peter, realizing his dietary freedom and the unity of the body of Christ, had begun to have close fellowship with Gentile believers, including having meals with them. That meant that Peter was probably eating that which was not in the prescribed Jewish diet. Even Barnabas had begun to enjoy these reconciliation barbecues. But when a group of Jewish believers came to town, Peter and all the other Jewish believers in Antioch—who apparently took their cue from him—immediately halted these pork-fests. Peter's actions were inconsistent. The New American Standard translation says that Paul called them "hypocrisy" (v. 13). When such a prominent leader as Peter was hypocritical, it sent the wrong message to both Gentiles and Jews, namely, that the unity of those in Christ is an important truth worth teaching but it is less important for our daily living. Paul could not accept this hypocritical behavior because he knew that people would eventually follow the actions of a leader. For this reason Paul took the strong step of confronting Peter "in the presence of all" to correct this dangerous error.

Yet we can relate to Peter and the other Jewish believers of Antioch, can't we? It is difficult to consistently follow what we say we believe. To live a life that attempts to love people regardless of their race is difficult. It is rarely understood or appreciated. I have been told that our church would be a better place for black visitors if we did not have whites present. I have also seen white visitors walk out of our services after meeting me and seeing that the majority of our church is black. These are the hardest times for me to live out my conviction on multiracial ministry, but these are also the best times for they have taught me commitment to the vision God has laid on my heart.

Being a Friend

Getting personally involved in the life of someone from a different ethnic group is one of the best ways to get beyond the stereotypes we are all taught. With a friend you can have frank conversations that will make you aware of the issues and differing viewpoints affecting the other person's life. You also will begin to understand, although to a limited degree, how others see you and the society in which you live. Many leaders don't understand the issues that separate the races and this hinders their ability to address the concerns of their followers. But if you make an effort to get to know people who are different from you, your awareness of their concerns will be heightened.

To be fully committed and to have success in this ministry, a leader must be passionate about reconciliation. A half-hearted commitment will accomplish little and may eventually work against you because you will find it at cross-purposes with other goals. Give yourself wholeheartedly to racial reconciliation. This ministry may be fragile and often attacked but its value is beyond measure, so diligently prepare for it, carry it out wisely, and guard its value. One of the ways this value can be diminished is by allowing careless words and deeds to wrongly portray that you are prejudiced. Because I have seen this happen to others, I have chosen not to say anything, even in jest, that might be taken as my speaking against another racial group. This is a rule I hold to in my private as well as public interactions with others.

Pastors Arthur Johnson of Doers of the Word Church and David Wooten of New Life Assembly of God in Alabama have modeled the committed lives that are needed to have the ministry of racial reconciliation become the passion of a church. Pastor Johnson shared that he sought out a white pastor with the purpose of initiating and developing a relationship with him. The strategy would be to begin by praying with this pastor, later to have their wives meet, then to have dinner together in each family's home, to become accountable to each other, and to eventually have their churches worship together every fifth Sunday. Pastor Johnson stated, "I was trying to model how a person can be intentional about the ministry of racial reconciliation." Later when he met Pastor Wooten at a local Promise Keepers planning session, he began a relationship that has seen Pastor Johnson accomplish his goals of modeling racial reconciliation and has seen Pastor Wooten's church be actively involved in supporting his friend's church. This is also fulfilling a goal that David Wooten has been passionate about since becoming involved in Promise Keepers.

Set Their Hearts on Fire and Their Feet in Motion

As a leader, and especially if you are a pastor, you have the great opportunity to give those under your leadership guidance on how to reach out and love others beyond those differences that separate us. Yes, we do have to teach our people how to love others who are of a different racial group because reconciliation is a very uncommon and seemingly unnatural concept in our sinful world. We will have to introduce our people to the reconciliation way of life and then guide them in understanding how they can live it out. First, we teach them, setting their hearts on fire, and then we walk them, setting their feet in motion, into this way of life.

To set their hearts on fire, we must communicate our passion. Some people seem to have more success than others in communicating a message. As the old saying goes: "When so and so speaks, we clap. But when so and so speaks, we go to war!" Now, we may not have the communication skills to convince people to go to war, but to communicate our passion, we don't need special skill. Passion is part of our mind and emotions and when we talk to people, whatever we're passionate about will be obvious. It's true that the greater a person's passion, the more he or she will talk about it. Often people will keep on talking about what excites them because they hope others will get as excited. Somehow every conversation gets back to their passion. With this repetition comes influence, the ability to influence the thoughts and emotions of others so that they adopt the view of the passionate person. If leaders therefore desire to see the hearts of others set on fire for the ministry of racial reconciliation, they must repeatedly talk about their commitment to this ministry, its value, its importance, and its goal.

The Old Testament gives us a wonderful testimony of this method's importance in Deuteronomy 6:4–9. Here we are told that those who were committed to serving the true and living God were to express that commitment by constantly talking, applying, and teaching God's Word ("you shall teach them diligently . . . talk of them . . . bind them as a sign . . . you shall write them on the doorposts"). Clearly the passion of these committed followers was to be communicated through every aspect of their lives so that it would catch fire in the hearts of those who came into contact with them. Such is the challenge for every leader with a passion. We must move our people to make this burning focus of ours their focus as well. It must become their passion and vision, for this will determine our overall effectiveness and success.

After setting their hearts on fire, we must set their feet in motion, which demands practical instruction that can be readily applied to the lives of our followers. Society has done a much better job of giving practical instruction than has the church. The military, state and federal governments, and almost all corporations and universities have diversity sensitivity classes and workshops on majority-minority relations. Their purpose is to show their people what they must do to create and maintain harmony in the workplace or classroom. Christian organizations must also instruct our people in practical ways to reach out to people and show them the love of Jesus.

In the church there are numerous ways this can be achieved. For example, Sunday school lessons, sermons, and "Invite a Friend Sunday" are all avenues that can be used to teach that the outreach of a reconciled life and ministry can take different forms and approaches. At our church, Grace Bible Fellowship, I taught a Sunday school series titled "Grace on Race." In this class we gave suggestions of ways in which our people could reach out to individuals of other racial groups. Pastor Samuel Reeves of Madison Avenue Christian Reformed Church has implemented annual reconciliation training sessions for the staff and leadership of his church.

Please remember that it is most important that this topic be preached and taught before the body is challenged through a racial emergency. Setbacks will be a lot easier to face if the people have already been told to expect them. Otherwise they may take a conflict as an indication that their endeavor cannot be achieved. The very history of our country teaches us that racial disunity is one of the most powerful and treasured weapons in Satan's arsenal. Why then should we expect Satan to give up on wielding this prized weapon because we have chosen to live racially reconciled lives? On the contrary, he'll use everything he's got to discourage and dissuade us.

Select Your Best Warriors

In the early and exciting days of the church's growth, a major opportunity for disaster arose that stands as a great lesson for leadership in a multiethnic context. We looked at this crisis in chapter 8. It is recorded in Acts 6 where we see the early church dealing with an ethnic issue not on the basis of ethnicity or race (an earthly perspective) but on the basis of grace (a spiritual perspective).

> Now at this time while the disciples were increasing in number, a complaint arose on the part of the Hellenistic Jews against the native Hebrews, because their widows were being overlooked in the daily serving of food. And the twelve summoned the congregation of the disciples and said, "It is not desirable for us to neglect the word of God in order to serve tables. But select from among you, brethren, seven men of good reputation, full of the Spirit and of wisdom, whom we may put in charge of this task. But we will devote ourselves to prayer, and to the ministry of the word." And the statement found approval with the whole congregation; and they chose Stephen, a man full of faith and of the Holy Spirit, and Philip, Prochorus, Nicanor, Timon, Parmenas and Nicolas, a proselyte from Antioch.
>
> Acts 6:1–5

The highlight of this passage is the approach taken by the leaders, the twelve apostles, in rectifying the problem. Note that these leaders neutralized this ethnic powder keg by directing that men who had strong spiritual, personal, and sensitivity qualifications should be chosen.

First, the men who were selected had outstanding spiritual qualifications. The apostles realized that the source of ethnic or racial problems and disharmony is sin and for that reason they addressed this situation by placing *godly warriors* on the front line. Please don't miss the important point that they intentionally chose godly individuals to wait on tables in the midst of a majority-minority conflict. If these men had to be greatly committed to God and holy to serve tables, how can we select those of lesser standards to work on the front lines in reconciliation situations today?

Second, individuals were chosen who had some of the *best* personal reputations, the cream of the crop of their numbers to meet the needs of these minority members. The leaders of the early church realized that those who were overlooked needed to be reassured of their importance to the congregation. For this reason the apostles were very intentional in their direction to select the best of the congregation to be assigned to meet the need. They could not have selected any man who was halfhearted in his commitment to God and in his interactions with others because his selection would have indicated to the minorities that the leaders had little concern for them. They wanted the best because they were striving to preserve the unity of the faith by not allowing bad feelings to grow. If the men they selected had to have such great character traits to serve tables, how can we select those of lesser character to work in reconciliation situations today?

Third, individuals from the *same* ethnic or racial group as the people in need of attention were chosen. This is a very important point because this move neutralized the feelings of those who could have said that individuals who were not concerned about their needs had been selected. Such a criticism could not be made because these men were of their own numbers and presumably would not be biased against their own people. The approach of the apostles in selecting minorities to meet the needs of minorities should not be viewed as arguing for a homogeneous-unit approach to ministry. The conflict mandated that the minorities in the body be assured that their concerns were highly important to the apostles. Their remedy met the need while preserving the unity of the multiethnic body.

The application of this action to our present ministry opportunities means that we will need to assure that both minority and majority people are in positions of leadership in organizations. The effect will be the communication of the ministry's commitment to racial reconciliation to both the majority and minority groups in the church and community. Again I ask, if men of such exemplary character were selected to serve tables, how can we select those of lesser character to work in reconciliation situations today?

Such a selection was made by Pastor Joey Johnson of The House of the Lord. He believed that adding a white pastor to the church's all-black pastoral staff was not an attempt to orchestrate the church's ethnic integration but an act of obedience to God's leading. "A lot of whites came when Pastor Bill [Mitchell] came on board. I didn't see how it was going to work and I don't believe that I am able to control the bringing of whites into our church. But because of my act of obedience in bringing Pastor Bill on staff, we now have about 20 percent of our total attendance in the church that is white."

To challenge those in his church who did not accept Pastor Bill, Pastor Joey periodically presented his position on racial reconciliation through sermons, emphasizing Jesus' design for his church. Pastor Joey has also placed Pastor Bill over certain ministry responsibilities, such as premarital counseling, and has mandated that those seeking these ministries must go to Pastor Bill, thus thwarting the attempts of some members to avoid interacting with him.

Pastor Michael Posey echoes this same commitment to representative leadership when he says, "When I am asked to assess if a church desires to be multiracial, I first request to look at its leadership. If they are not multiracial in their leadership, they are probably not committed to being a multiracial church." Pastor Posey went on to state, "To have a multiracial church and leadership means that a church must develop both white and black leaders to make them ready to lead."

The decision to place our best warriors on the front line to deal with race issues is necessary in light of Satan's response to our ministry. Our leaders must be prepared and ready for attacks that are sure to come. Satan will not be pleased if he sees that racism, the prized weapon of his arsenal, is losing its punch.

Be Innovative

One of the most precious gifts the Lord has given us is the ability to reflect his creativity, his ability to create something new to accomplish a desired goal. Unfortunately innovation is a gift that is greatly underutilized in most churches. Many times the church of Jesus Christ is more focused on reusing old wineskins than on creating innovative approaches to addressing today's problems, especially the wrongs of society, particularly in respect to race. In a ministry of racial reconciliation, there is much demand for innovation, especially in encouraging fellowship among a church's or organization's members and including various worship styles in a church's worship service.

Encouraging Interaction

One of my favorite word pictures that the Lord uses to describe his church is that of a human body. In describing us as one body, Jesus is strongly emphasizing the great need we each have for other believers, other members of his body. As cells must be in contact with one another to gain and transmit life-sustaining nutrients, so our interactions, especially those that go beyond general niceties, are necessary to provide the Holy Spirit with an important avenue for helping believers grow and thus building up Christ's body. For this reason, it is important for a leader to encourage the church's membership to draw closer to one another. Then the overall life and ministry of that church will be enhanced. But it takes innovation to come up with new ways that don't seem staged and artificial to encourage such interaction.

Pastor Joey notes both the need and the aim of such an innovation: "If there is anything that I would orchestrate, it would be some sort of mechanism to bring our people closer together. I see it happening on a small scale but we need more. Because they have fellowship does not mean that they have a relationship."

Pastor Arthur Johnson and Victor Powell, an elder at Doers of the Word, initiated what is called "Wednesday Night Stew." Pastor Johnson has found that blacks and whites have to deal with two different issues that affect their interactions. "Whereas blacks have to address feelings of inferiority in their interactions with whites, whites have to address feelings of superiority. Neither of these feelings are valid in Christ because the cross levels the playing field. If people have brought these feelings into the church, it will play itself out in different ways. Blacks will feel that to worship with whites is a step up while whites will feel that to worship with blacks is a step down."

The purpose of the "Stew" is to allow the "Recipe for Reconciliation," as Pastor Arthur Johnson describes it, to draw both groups together in a way that honors Christ. The recipe is:

1. *Know who you are in Christ.* This is achieved through honest and open discussions.
2. *Establish covenant relationships across racial lines.* Leadership purposefully matches up black and white couples to encourage them to fellowship and grow in a deeper knowledge of each other.
3. *Talk about the tough issues that divide us.* Topics such as interracial marriages, affirmative action, and the role

of government in urban issues are presented to the group for their honest interaction.

Pastor Johnson goes on to note that the integration being attempted in our society is often unsuccessful because all the focus is on number 3 in the recipe without having established the important foundation that only comes by working through numbers 1 and 2.

With the help of the Chicago Urban Reconciliation Enterprise (CURE), Pastor Reeves of Madison Square implemented the "Breakfast Club" program.[2] The program works to bridge the racial divide by encouraging church leaders and members of different races to meet monthly for breakfast and to intentionally interact over the issue of race. The commitment to have such meetings is for one year and the purpose of these meetings is to create sensitivity and an atmosphere that God can use to draw individuals of different racial backgrounds into permanent personal relationships. Over the twelve-month period CURE provides worksheets, questions, and articles to help guide discussions that will probe the intellectual and emotional issues of race.

Pastor Michael Posey has taken a more personal approach to drawing his church together. He mentioned that one of the actions that he continually undertakes is to talk openly about race and cultural issues. "I have learned from previous experience that you must continually talk on the subject and create an environment where it is safe for *everyone* to voice their opinion and to talk about issues freely. Whites must have the environment to be free to speak without being branded a racist."

At Grace Bible Fellowship we have implemented various innovations to encourage interaction between our members. The Body Life Ministry seeks to accomplish this goal by placing the members of Grace Bible Fellowship into planned fellowship events to foster deeper relationships and interaction than are possible on Sunday mornings. Its purpose is to coordinate relaxed and fun events that allow members and visitors an opportunity to come together and get to know one another better. One Body Life event that has worked well to enhance interaction despite racial differences is Dinner Groups.

For two to three Sundays each year Dinner Groups are promoted and everyone is encouraged to sign up to be a part of a group. Couples and singles do not select a group but are intentionally placed into a group comprised of three couples or six individuals with differing racial backgrounds. The groups meet for the next three months at the homes of different group members who take turns providing a main dish, a side dish, and a dessert. Questions are provided to the groups to foster discussion. We have had enthusiastic responses from these dinners and have seen ongoing relationships develop because of them.

Encouraging Inclusion in Worship

The aspect of ministry that is most often mentioned as a challenge for bringing people of different races together in the same church is worship. Individuals, especially those from different ethnic groups, have different likes and dislikes in respect to musical styles, preaching styles, and appropriate audience response. Yet we must remember that the challenge of bringing people together in worship exists even in churches comprised of one racial group. This point was brought to my attention while speaking at a pastors' conference on the subject of racial reconciliation in the local church. As I began to discuss the need to have various worship traditions represented in the morning service, an older pastor raised his hand and asked permission to say a few words. With a smile on his face he told us that he had seven different churches in the church he pastored. I was bewildered but waited a few minutes hoping that he would clarify his statement. He went on to say that he had seven different choirs in his church that presented seven different types of musical styles from black spirituals to more contemporary gospel songs. He has come to learn that each one of those choirs appeals to a different group in the church and therefore has a separate following among the church's membership. Therefore the church receives calls on a Sunday morning inquiring as to which choir will be singing that morning. Depending on the choir that is singing, the callers determine if they will attend the morning service in time to hear the choir.

Clearly the challenge presented by various worship-style preferences in the same church is to create a moving worship experience that blends rather than isolates the various worship traditions. When we intentionally accept and represent racial and ethnic differences in a church, and by so doing magnify the oneness of believers in Christ (inHimtegration), we also create the need for blending of worship styles.

> There is a movement among the people of the world to find out about each other's traditions and to share from each other's experiences. We the people of the church have even more reason to learn what is happening in other worship cultures and to draw from each other's spiritual insights and experiences. After all, there is only one church, and although there are a variety of traditions and experiences within this church, each tradition is indeed part of the whole. The movement toward the convergence of worship traditions and the spiritual stimulation which comes with borrowing from various worship communities are the results of the worship renewal taking place in our time.[3]

At Grace we have attempted to implement a blended approach to worship. In a typical worship service our singing will flow from a hymn to a gospel classic to a worship chorus to a contemporary Christian song. The comments that I hear are overall very positive, although there are those who have requested more of one style in the worship because that is their preference.

There is an important caution that must be sounded at this point, for not all leaders who are involved in interracial ministries would agree that pastors must take an intentional role in leading their churches. One such pastor is Jim Cymbala who believes that it should not be the primary goal of pastors or church leaders to take steps to achieve racial reconciliation. Rather, he believes that as a church focuses on following Jesus and being obedient to the Holy Spirit, God will then bring individuals of different racial and cultural backgrounds together. God's love working through us will accomplish what needs to be done.

Jim Cymbala says, "I never think, *What can I do to pull people of different racial backgrounds into our church? Or, What can I do to keep them?* The minute you do anything to bring about this goal, you grieve away the Holy Spirit. Talk the way you usually talk, preach Jesus, and be natural. I can't imagine Jesus acting any other way than the way he is. Peter Jennings just acts and speaks as he presents himself on television. Unfortunately, Peter Jennings is more real than many pastors who put on cultural airs in order to appeal to others. In so doing they attempt to bring about a spiritual goal through unspiritual means. The key to achieving everything God desires is in being *open* to the power of the Holy Spirit."

Be Persistent!

Michael Posey noted that a primary reason why pastors don't lead their churches to be multiracial or why many pastors give up in this pursuit is that they select the easy route over the biblical route. "We are so content to have large churches and we are so content in our own success, but when you outline your target person you gear the ministry to attract that type of person. But to a degree it is like fishing with a line rather than fishing with a net. The only time Jesus commanded his disciples to fish with a line was when they were going after money."

Curtiss DeYoung notes that reconciliation is a holistic ministry. He counsels that leaders must seek the face of God because they will need "the ability to exist in situations where they are confronted by a multiplicity of challenges, situations where they will have to accurately discern the various dynamics that confront them and be able to do this on various levels of their ministry." Such a leadership outlook demands that the leader realize the difficulty of this ministry and that it cannot be accomplished through his or her own strength or wisdom. Such realism must also move the leader to prepare others in leadership positions for the difficulties that lie ahead of them. Disappointed idealism must not be allowed to sap the energy of those involved in this ministry. Otherwise, when leaders encounter the extent of the difficulties often involved in reconciliation ministry, they will be tempted to quit. As DeYoung notes, "Reconciliation is about *process,* and all involved must be prepared for a long-term commitment."

Clearly the ministry of racial reconciliation is a challenging task that will stretch any leader involved in it. Yet, as has been pointed out by the leaders who were interviewed in this chapter, there is also a great sense of purpose that results from experiencing the racial and cultural unity God ordained for his universal church and expects of its local manifestations. For this reason, the church is compelled to exhibit its multiracial, multinational, and multicultural character. Pastor and scholar John Stott beautifully highlights this truth:

> There has been considerable debate in recent years whether a local church could or should ever be culturally homogeneous. A consultation [the Pasadena Report] on this issue concluded that no church should ever acquiesce in such a condition: "All of us are agreed that in many situations a

homogeneous unit church can be a legitimate and authentic church. Yet we are also agreed that it can never be complete in itself. Indeed, if it remains in isolation, it cannot reflect the universality and diversity of the Body of Christ. Nor can it grow to maturity. Therefore every homogeneous unit church must take active steps to broaden its fellowship in order to demonstrate visibly the unity and the variety of Christ's Church."[4]

Still, the key factor in achieving this goal is leadership, for everything rises and falls with leadership.

ELEVEN

ALL FOR ONE

We are caught in an inescapable network of mutuality,
tied in a single garment of destiny.

Dr. Martin Luther King Jr.

My prayer is that after reading this book you will have
understood two basic truths: Racial reconciliation is not
an option for Christians and racial reconciliation is
never easy. God has called each of us to be reconciled
to others in his body and he has promised, as with everything else he commands us to do, that he will help us
accomplish it. I hope that the biblical teaching, the historical examples, and our contemporary challenges
have convinced you that as a Christian leader or layperson, you want to be involved in this crucial ministry.

Let me give you some final words of encouragement,
taken from my own experience in pursuing racial reconciliation with all my brothers and sisters in Christ:
Racial reconciliation doesn't just happen. Those who
wish to pursue it must do so intentionally. They must
not step out without becoming informed about the history of the other group. Then they must be ready to
extend and receive forgiveness. They must drop all the

old stereotypes and they must be prepared to stand alone in their convictions and against the criticism of others. This is what God expects. This is what he has called us to do.

Practice Intentionality

Intentional action in respect to race relations is hard to accept by those who do not see the ministry of reconciliation as a central part of the gospel and the Christian's responsibility. But for those who are committed to this ministry, there is no way to respond other than by making it an intentional practice or priority in their lives. Let's face it. We are intentional about those things we deem important. If we desire to obtain an objective or a goal, such as a raise or an academic degree, we become singleminded in our pursuit of that goal. Our motivation is the belief that the desired results are worth our intentional actions. The desired result of seeing the gospel of Jesus Christ magnified through its transcendence of racial disunity in America is a great goal that deserves our purposeful activity.

There is no better measure of our practicing intentionality than our approach to evangelism. We evangelical Christians are very intentional when it comes to identifying individuals or groups of people with whom we desire to communicate the gospel. We will go out of our way, even cultivating new interests or sometimes moving to a new location to establish relationships with these individuals. Then when these relationships are strengthened, they allow us to communicate the gospel in a nonthreatening manner. Unfortunately we don't have the same perspective when it comes to pursuing friendships with individuals of another race or culture in order to impact their lives and to allow them the opportunity to impact ours. Often, when this concept of intentional reconciliation is suggested, the response is, "But that seems insincere." The truth is, however, that if we don't make an effort to establish relationships with people different from us, they just don't happen. Raleigh Washington and Glen Kehrein note that although blacks and whites interact with one another on a daily basis, what they call "circumstantial integration," this interaction does not guarantee that deeper relationships will result. They note that only when individuals intentionally go outside of their comfort zones to include others and to address barriers between them are deeper relationships fostered.[1] Please note that this approach was used by our Savior who intentionally went into Samaria to interact with a woman for the purpose of achieving spiritual and racial (ethnic) reconciliation (John 4:4).

On the basis of our Savior's example it is important that we commit to making the ministry of reconciliation a part of our own lives and ministry. One of the best ways to begin or deepen your personal commitment to the ministry of racial reconciliation is to intentionally pray for God to prepare you and to direct you in this endeavor. Then seek to identify someone, or a group of people, of a different racial group with whom you will begin to establish a relationship. The next step is to initiate contact. Individuals who wish to initiate contact could join an activity group, such as a health spa or book club, to meet different people, or they could take a coworker or neighbor out to lunch. Groups can initiate contact with diverse people groups through working in a ministry, such as a city's rescue mission or Habitat for Humanity. As you develop a close relationship with others of a different racial group, you will begin to understand them and learn what is important to them. Yet the benefit is not just that you will learn more about others, for you will also come to learn more about yourself.

When my wife and I came to North Carolina as independent church planters, I wanted to make sure that I had a group of men who would hold me accountable. In considering individuals for this board I intentionally selected a group that was evenly divided along racial lines. I wanted the insight of both groups of men to make sure that from its inception the church planting endeavor would be true to its stated goal of starting an interracial church. It was not long before I realized that, although the counsel of board members did not always agree, they provided important insights from differing cultural perspectives. For example, as I contemplated whether I should go full-time or continue to pastor in a bivocational capacity, I was able to merge the counsel of black pastors, who were used to a bivocational ministry model, with that of white pastors, who were used to a full-time ministry model. This experience stretched me beyond an "either/or" approach to this and other issues in our church to a "both/and" approach.

Know Before You Go

Before attempting to become an agent of reconciliation it is absolutely essential that we first realize that people from different ethnic groups hold different perspectives on race. We will deal here in particular with the perspective held by most whites and blacks. These perspectives can be found in Christians as well as non-Christians of both racial groups. Before reading this section, I suggest that you first reread the opening story of chapter 5.

White Christians Must Understand

The Christian who is white and seeks to reach out to someone who is black must understand the pain and resultant anger that resides within the black community. The intensity of these emotions varies but their presence is understandable when one considers the history of sin's manifestation through racial hatred in America. A major challenge to racial reconciliation being realized is that most white Americans do not consider that the history of oppression and discrimination in America is relevant for race relations today.

"The past is behind us," is the outlook many whites have toward America's race history. But the past is very relevant to most African Americans.

For this reason, it is very insensitive for someone who is white to brush aside the wrongs of the past as irrelevant and insignificant to race relations today. One of the first things a black person will seek to know when coming into any meaningful interaction with a white person—for some African Americans this is true in any contact with whites—is whether that person understands and can empathize with the struggles African Americans have endured in America.[2] This does not mean that every African American is demanding an apology from every white American, but it means that African Americans still know and feel the pain such knowledge of the past brings. Therefore let me reemphasize that calling America's race history irrelevant for interactions between whites and blacks today is insensitive and will not be well received.

Although the sins of white America are forgiven in Christ, there are scars that remain within the minds of African Americans that must be acknowledged and dealt with sensitively. Sure, most white Americans would not consider themselves racists and would decry America's discriminatory past. But many would argue that they should not have to be repentant for wrongs that members of their racial group committed in the past. Yet there are three strong counterarguments to this position. First, many of those who make this argument have no reservations about taking pride in the historic and contemporary achievements of members of groups with which they identify (such as their country, university, church, or racial group). To share in the accomplishments of those groups mandates that individuals be willing to share in their wrongs as well. For that reason it is erroneous for individuals to think that they can identify only with the accomplishments of the South when they brandish the Confederate flag, a matter of "heritage" the bumper sticker states, without correspondingly being identified with the hate that flag also represented.

A second reason that whites cannot absolve themselves from being identified with the racial wrongs in America is that we all bear a moral association to sins we benefit from, although we may not have committed these sins ourselves. If we did not commit a wrong or profit from it, we would then have no association with that wrong. But that is not the case in respect to race, as whites in America continue to benefit from favorable stereotypes and expectations that work to their advantage, since they are still more likely to meet another white person when pursuing a job, house, bank loan, or a judicial decision.[3] On the other hand, African Americans continue to struggle because of a history of negative stereotypes and expectations that are still perpetuated.

Without understanding and accepting the pain that most blacks still feel, whites will find their attempts to establish relationships with African Americans doomed from their inception. But a sensitive appreciation for the feelings and mindset of blacks is good preparation for a white person who wants to be a minister of reconciliation. (See the suggested reading list for books that will increase your understanding.)

Black Christians Must Understand

The black Christian who seeks to reach out to a white person must understand that in the white community there is a pervasive lack of knowledge about blacks, their thoughts and issues. Although blacks are raised from a young age to live in two worlds—that of their black communities and that of the dominant white culture—whites are not. For this reason most blacks have a better understanding of white America than white America has of them. Because of this knowledge imbalance, whites will sometimes act standoffish because they are not sure what to say or do, and many times they will say things that can be taken as insensitive.

Pastor Michael Posey relates that he has gone to his denomination's meetings, where whites predominated, and people would not speak to him. He at first thought the reason for this was that they were racists but later learned that they did not speak to him because they didn't know what to say or were afraid that they would say the wrong thing. "Blacks must realize that it's not always the case that whites don't want you around them; it's that they don't know what to do with you."

"They should know better" is the response many blacks would give to such instances, but the ministry of racial reconciliation demands a more loving response.

Any black person who seeks to minister to someone who is white must approach the task with understanding and a commitment to extend grace. Such an approach demands that blacks not interpret every questionable act or word as a manifestation of racism. Instead they must be willing to extend to these individuals the benefit of the doubt. This is a very difficult step to take in light of the pervasive feelings many blacks have that most, if not all, whites are racists who must be shown the error of their ways. Therefore, they expect whites to be insensitive, for this is how racist individuals act and speak.

The extent to which African Americans realize the breadth of white America's lack of knowledge about blacks will determine their desire to extend grace. I know this to be true and had to apply this approach while I was teaching a seminary class on race relations. During one class a student asked why slavery was such a hard issue for African Americans to get beyond. What he was really saying was, "Why is slavery so hard for your race to get over?" The student went on to say that he had always thought of slavery as a war between two groups and that one group, blacks, were defeated and for that reason they suffered the penalty of this outcome, enslavement.

I must tell you that this approach to slavery was very new to me and not only did it catch me off guard, but it also raised some emotions in me that wanted to respond to this seemingly racist statement. For in this student's mind the defeat of blacks in "the war" was a valid justification for slavery. Fortunately I realized that if I was going to have an influence in the lives of this individual and his classmates, I could not denigrate him with a flippant response that would show the absurdity of such a perspective. Instead I took the time to explain that there had never been a military conflict between Africans and Americans. The enslavement of Africans in America was not the result of a war but occurred because whites adopted a view that blacks were inferior in order to benefit economically from their mistreatment. To view slavery as just the natural result of a defeat in war is to remove the sin and culpability of whites in America.

After I patiently explained this, the student was able to see the difference between his perspective and that of most African Americans. I later heard from various students in the class that they appreciated the freedom I gave the students to ask tough questions and my sensitivity to their lack of knowledge.

For African Americans to be in a position to not allow our emotions to guide our responses, we must get rid of our anger. This can only be done by covering the wrongs of the past through biblical forgiveness. The term *forgiveness* is not very popular when applied to the wrongs of slavery and discrimination, but it is a necessity. Let us examine what biblical forgiveness truly is and how it can be applied to the reconciliation of blacks and whites.

Forgiveness Is a Choice

One of the greatest, if not the greatest, challenges in trying to reconcile a marriage where both members have committed various offenses against the other is to get them to forgive each other. A major hindrance in achieving this goal is the response, "I can't forgive because I can't forget what was done." But forgetting is not the basis of true biblical forgiveness. At this point I am sure that some may be wondering how I could make such a statement in light of the "biblical mandate" to forgive and forget. So let us look at that mandate. First, the Bible does not tell us that forgetting is a prerequisite of forgiveness. In contrast, biblical forgiveness is a choice to forgive someone because we understand the greatness of God's forgiveness of us through the work of Jesus Christ (Eph. 4:32; Luke 7:36–50). This choice is not to be based on our ability or inability to forget the offense. Although songs are sung about God's placing our sins in the "sea of forgetfulness," the Bible is clear that God knows all things, which negates his ability to forget. Rather, God's forgiveness is first based on his *choice* to forgive us and secondly on his choice to not respond to us with the anger and judgment our offense deserves (Ps. 103:12; 1 John 1:9).

Some people would say that because African Americans must forgive white Americans, they should try to forget about slavery and the wrongs of the past. But because forgiveness does not demand that the offense be forgotten, I believe that African Americans should continue to learn about slavery and to teach their children about this period of our history, emphasizing the greatness of God in bringing their ancestors through the bondage to deliverance. I do not believe that African Americans need to forget and play down what occurred because it may cause whites to feel uncomfortable. Consider that God commanded Israel to remember their bondage under the Egyptians for all generations (Exod. 13:3; Deut. 5:15), even though he knew that Egyptians would someday become his worshipers (Deut. 23:7–8). Still, the Jews were to allow their captivity and deliverance to motivate their commitment to Yahweh because of what he had done for them, but they were not to hold animosity toward the Egyptians. So slavery must be remembered by African Americans, not as a basis for separation from and animosity toward whites but as the basis for a deeper commitment to God, actually moving them to actively love a group that formerly oppressed them.

As much as biblical forgiveness is not based on our ability to forget, it is also not based on our ability to feel an emotional bond with the person forgiven. I mention this misconception because both blacks and whites who have been offended by members of another racial group may oppose truly forgiving those individuals because they don't feel comfortable around them. This would be a valid counterargument to our responsibility to forgive those who have offended us if it were not for the fact that God never even considers our feelings in his commands for us to forgive those who offend us. An important reason for this omission is the fact that our feelings will not always agree with the actions God has called us to undertake. The key point here is that we make the choice to act in accordance with God's will in spite of how we feel. Booker T. Washington, who was born and spent his early years in slavery, noted the importance of making the choice to forgive those who hurt you:

> I would permit no man, no matter what his colour might be, to narrow and degrade my soul by making me hate him. With God's help, I believe that I have completely rid myself of any ill feeling toward the Southern white man for any wrong that he may have inflicted upon my race. . . . I pity from the bottom of my heart any individual who is so unfortunate as to get into the habit of holding race prejudice.[4]

There are wrongs on both sides of the race aisle. Yet God's command is clear that all Christians must make forgiveness such a part of their lifestyle that it eventually comes to characterize our lives and our interactions with others.

Drop the Stereotypes

In its most basic meaning a stereotype is a general fact or belief that we hold about our world. For this reason, stereotypes influence our everyday lives. From a young age we are taught to understand and operate within our world through stereotypes along with basic principles that are to guide our lives and our interaction with others. For example, we are all taught the basic principle that when we meet someone for the first time an extended hand is an invitation to shake hands. Because stereotypes can be based on facts as well as beliefs, which may or may not be accurate, stereotypes can have negative as well as positive effects on us.

In respect to race, stereotypes are overstated beliefs about a classification of people that may or may not be accurate. They are developed when a person identifies a characteristic that he or she notices about an individual, or a few individuals, and then attaches that trait to the person's racial group. For example, the observation that most rap artists are black might lead a person to hold the stereotype that all blacks like rap music. Or the observation that most classical composers are white may lead a person to wrongly stereotype all whites as liking classical music. Obviously these are two stereotypes that may be true in some cases, but are not true in all cases.

Stereotypes become most dangerous when they give us a negative or uncomplimentary image of members of a racial or ethnic group. These negative stereotypes can be the source of and justification for negative treatment of a group of people or its individual members. This is evident in the teachings of many white supremacy groups, such as the Aryan warriors who teach that blacks, Jews, and anyone supporting them are inherently evil—"disciples of Satan."[5] This is also evident in the teachings of many black groups such as the Nation of Islam that teaches that whites are inherently evil—devils. On a more common level, racial stereotypes are a part of our everyday lives in that they are communicated and reinforced through jokes told by family members, experiences described by friends, and the actions of characters on television sitcoms.

One of the best ways to counter the tendency to relate to people according to our stereotypes of them is to commit ourselves to treating people as individuals. When we meet a person and assume that we know a lot about him or her based on our knowledge of the racial group, we are setting ourselves up to be embarrassed. Therefore, take the time to get to know the person and never make assumptions about what he or she will be like.

The effect of stereotypes on a ministry can be very subtle, and for this reason much alertness needs to be given to recognizing and addressing them. I can think of one such situation and the sad result when I failed to do so. One day during a leadership meeting, one of the participants mentioned that he felt we should not have only whites counting the money after service because this played into the common view of blacks that whites are usually behind the scenes in positions of power and "handling" the money. I knew that this was a common view in the black community but I did not want to make a change just to keep from perpetuating this stereotype. Still, the other group member, who was white, thought that this was an impression we did not want to give. Since he was one of the two individuals who counted the offering after the service, I gave in and decided to ask the woman who was doing that task to step out of this role and into another. I knew she was offended when I did not see her or her husband the Sunday after I had spoken with her. Sure enough, that was the case. She had taken offense at my request and saw it as a clear breach in my commitment to having an interracial church. No matter how much I explained the rationale for the change or that the white male had supported this decision, she remained deeply hurt and disappointed. Even though she accepted my sincere apology, she never really forgave me and later left the church citing this event as a primary reason for her choice.

Of all the decisions I have made as a pastor that I regret, this stands at the top of the list. I was not alert enough to recognize how my action would appear—that I too held the stereotype—when in fact I was trying to protect the church from criticism by those who really did hold this view. Now I know that if I had resisted the change, thereby challenging those who held the stereotype to confront their bias, the outcome would have been more positive.

Prepare to Stand Alone

Anyone who chooses to make racial reconciliation a major part of his or her life must make a commitment to walk alone, if necessary. There must be a determination to love those of another racial group, even though members of our own racial group, within and outside the body of Christ, condemn us. As a person who experienced the sting of taking a stand for truth, Martin Luther King Jr. reminds us that every person is committed to a cause. We must make sure that we give our lives to the highest cause possible.

> In that dramatic scene on Calvary's hill three men were crucified. We must never forget that all three were crucified for the same crime—the crime of extremism. Two were extremists for immorality, and thus fell below their environment. The other, Jesus Christ, was an extremist for love, truth and goodness, and thereby rose above his environment.[6]

As I read Scripture, I am always amazed by the consistency of Jesus' stance for truth and righteousness, even when it caused him to become more and more isolated. Often Jesus could have strayed from the goal God had set for him but he chose to lose followers rather than gain them for a goal he was not supposed to achieve. The focus of Jesus was far greater than the earthly kingdoms that were offered to him as alternatives to God's desire (Matt. 4:1–11), but his stand in agreement with God's will for him resulted in an isolation that eventually led to his lonely crucifixion at the hand of those he came to save. So also each Christian must choose to take a stand that will place God's desire over his or her own popularity and comfort.

Conclusion

Finally, please note a key principle that must guide our interracial interactions: *Let the offender be gracious and the offended compassionate.* The motivation that will allow us to get to the place where we can utilize this principle is the realization that we need each other. This is clearly presented in 1 Corinthians 12:12–27 where Paul expounds on the fact that diversity in the body of Christ is part of the Father's design. There are tremendous benefits that every member then gains when these differences are accepted and allowed to be used by the Holy Spirit for his goals.

Here are some important questions that can help guide us in our self-evaluation and our commitment to the ministry of racial reconciliation.

1. How serious am I about being involved in the ministry of racial reconciliation?

Not very serious   **Very serious**

1   2   3   4   5

2. What am I doing or not doing that would cause me to rate myself this way?

3. What hinders me from doing more?

4. What can I do to become more seriously involved in reaching out to others who are different from me? What will I read? Whom will I target? By what date? (I have given you an example.)

Goals	Starting Date	Specific Action
Enter into a cross-cultural relationship	December 2	Pray that God will identify the appropriate person

Lord, help me to be more totally yielded to your will and your desire for my life that I may be used as your instrument for spiritual and racial healing. Amen.

PASTORS INTERVIEWED FOR THIS BOOK

Jim Cymbala is the white senior pastor of the Brooklyn Tabernacle in Brooklyn, New York. He has been pastor of the church for more than twenty-five years and in that time the church has grown from twenty members to more than six thousand. Brooklyn Tabernacle is a church that is known for its commitment to prayer, interracial membership, and its world-renowned choir.

My conversation with Pastor Cymbala was very important for this book because although our views differed on an intentional approach to the ministry of racial reconciliation, his comments highlighted the danger of attempting to orchestrate a result that only God can provide. He said, "As we experience God through the power of the Holy Spirit, we will look at the world the way God looks at the world. When we emphasize our race or culture, we are then glorifying an accident of our birth. You did not choose to be black, white, American, et cetera. Others are boasting in the different colors of their skin or the countries they were born in. We need to be the spiritual people that God wants us to be, which will then transcend mere culture and color. We need to relate to people not after their flesh but after their spirit. The hearts of all people are the same and the truly spiritual ministry can relate and speak into the hearts of them all."

Such an approach is very much in line with Pastor Cymbala's passion for God and the emphasis of his ministry. Both of these are evident in his best-selling book *Fresh Wind, Fresh Fire,* which he authored with Dean Merrill.

Curtiss DeYoung is a white ordained minister in the Church of God of Anderson, Indiana, who pastored in Minneapolis, Minnesota, before becoming president of Twin Cities Urban Reconciliation Network (TURN). Reverend DeYoung pastored a multiracial church in the Minneapolis area for five years but is now a "lay pastor" at Park Avenue United Methodist Church in Minneapolis. His role as an advocate of racial reconciliation is so prominent in the congregation that he was recommended when I sought to speak to a pastor about Park Avenue's ministry of racial reconciliation.

Park Avenue United Methodist is over a hundred years old and originally served a rural neighborhood. Although a nearby high school had only four black students in its 1946 yearbook, change began in the 1950s, with the result that the Park Avenue neighborhood became inner city. Many of the church's members moved out of the area and commuted to church. Although this pattern is quite common across the country, Park Avenue United Methodist is uncommon because in 1973 the church chose to stay and reach out to its community. The decision to become multiracial caused many whites to leave, but the large departure of whites has since ceased.

Today Park Avenue United Methodist is a congregation of more than one thousand. Curtiss DeYoung notes, "In the last seven to ten years the church has become more focused on reconciliation and also more intentional. They initially embraced [racial reconciliation] and celebrated it without discussing or dialoguing about it. That dynamic was not dealt with. As more folks of color moved into leadership positions, how race impacts us as a multiracial church had to be further grappled with. The commitment to reconciliation just doesn't go away." Now the church has intentionally developed a multiracial staff and racial reconciliation is a part of the church's mission statement.

The commitment to racial reconciliation has always been prominent in the life of Curtiss DeYoung. From a young adult he has intentionally chosen to seek a "dual development" by learning the black milieu of ministry through ministerial experiences in black churches in Harlem and by attending seminary at historically black Howard University in Washington, D.C. After graduation he moved to Minneapolis to pastor a Church of God congregation that desired to become a multiracial ministry. He pastored the church for five years and learned a great deal about racial transition in a church. His commitment to reconciliation has led him to write on the subject in his two works: *Coming Together: The Bible's Message in an Age of Diversity* and *Reconciliation: Our Greatest Challenge, Our Only Hope.*

Arthur Johnson is the African American founder and pastor of Doers of the Word Church in Birmingham, Alabama. Pastor Johnson began the church in 1990 and the membership has reached 150 (60 percent black and 40 percent white). From its inception it was Pastor Johnson's desire to have the church be an interracial body like the Antioch Church in Acts 13.

The desire to achieve such a goal is rooted in Pastor Johnson's being raised in Birmingham and learning of its history as one of the most thoroughly segregated cities in the country during the Civil Rights movement of the 1950s and 1960s. It was here that Dr. Martin Luther King Jr. wrote his famous letter from the Birmingham jail and ninety miles away in Selma is where the infamous attack by the local police on a march by black children occurred. It came to be called "Bloody Sunday." Pastor Johnson's brother and several members of his congregation were actively involved in the Civil Rights movement, so the memories of that period are still very real to them.

Doers of the Word has a strong commitment to the ministry of racial reconciliation, manifested in the fact that "racial healing" is one of its eight ministry foci. One of the ways they pursue this goal is through a joint service with a predominantly white church every fifth Sunday. Overall, the primary objective of their ministry in respect to race is to dismantle the walls of racial hatred, prejudices, and ignorance in Birmingham. The reason for Pastor Johnson's strong commitment is, as he states, "The church is the only entity that is guaranteed victory. Not the government, not policy makers, but Jesus said that the gates of hell will not stand against the church."

Flanvis Josephus Johnson Jr., affectionately known by his congregation as Pastor Joey, is the African American founder and senior pastor of The House of the Lord, a nondenominational church in Akron, Ohio. Pastor Joey has seen The House of the Lord grow from an initial attendance in his parents' living room of four people in 1974 to a membership in 1999 of over four thousand.

From the inception of The House of the Lord it was the vision of Pastor Joey to meet God's desire for a church that lives out the unity and solidarity that is produced through the gospel, a church that would treat all people as equal and welcomed. Although The House of the Lord's growth has primarily been in the African American community, there has been a renewed commitment to the initial vision, which has seen white attendance grow to 20 percent of the church's overall attendance.

Michael Posey is the African American senior pastor of Church of the Harvest, a Foursquare Pentecostal Church in Evansville, Indiana. The Church of the Harvest is a one hundred–member church of about 50 percent black and 50 percent white, with Latinos just now beginning to attend. Pastor Posey has been at the church for two years, having left a large multiethnic church in the south suburb of Chicago, Illinois, where he served as assistant pastor. While at this large church he cowrote *Race & Reconciliation: Healing the Wounds, Winning the Harvest,* as part of the Spirit-Filled Life, Kingdom Dynamics Study Guide series edited by Jack Hayford.

Pastor Posey is not the founding pastor of Church of the Harvest and it was not started with the intent that it would be a multiracial church, although the founding pastor would be open to that result. Still, the Evansville area presents challenges for an interracial church. The city has had a history of Ku Klux Klan influence and racial segregation. Pastor Posey believes that racism today is a lot more covert in the community than it used to be but is still there. White members have confided in him that they would not want to tell their extended family that their pastor is black because it would be unacceptable to them.

Black members have found the church hard to categorize. There is a black senior pastor but the blended worship musical style is not what they've experienced before. They are also surprised that social and community issues are not emphasized. But the commitment of the members is strong. Pastor Posey says, "It comes to the point that this is who we are. The fact that we are multiracial always comes up but this is who we are. There will come a time when I and the ministry will be able to back away from race being so prominent in our ministry but we will hold to this commitment till then."

Samuel B. Reeves Jr. is an African (from the country of Liberia in West Africa) copastor of Madison Square Christian Reformed Church in Grand Rapids, Michigan. He pastors with David H. Beelen, who is white. Since the 1970s the church has been committed to operate under multiracial pastoral leadership and to be a multiracial ministry. Part of the church's mission statement reads:

Reach up to exalt God.
Reach in to build each other up in the faith.
Reach out to serve and witness to our community and the world.
Reach across to appreciate and celebrate our racial and cultural diversity.

Presently, Madison Square is a fifteen hundred-member church that is 70 percent white and 30 percent people of color (blacks, Latinos, Asians).

Coming to the church in 1997, Pastor Reeves is the third black pastor the church has had. The first of the two former black pastors ministered at the church for eighteen years before resigning because of the way he was treated by white Christian Reformed pastors from America while traveling and ministering with them in South Africa. The second pastor felt that his lack of formal theological education limited his effectiveness with white members and decided that it was best for him to move on.

Pastor Reeves comes to this ministry with a master of divinity degree from Princeton and, though he believes his degree has helped him in his ministry at the church, he believes that is not the only reason for the good support he has received from the white members. He stated that when he was recruited, he was told that his leadership would be a vital part of the work of the church. He sees his role as keeping the church's feet to the fire to live what they say they hold to in respect to racial reconciliation. He believes that although he has encountered some problems in his work at the church, overall he has received wide support in accomplishing his goal and that of the church.

David Wooten is the white senior pastor of New Life Assembly of God in Westover, Alabama. The church is fourteen years old and Pastor Wooten has been there for eight years. Although the church averages about 250 in attendance and is situated in a predominantly white community, with 98 percent of their members white, they have a growing passion to reach out to the predominantly black community that is about five miles away.

Pastor Wooten attributes the change in his life and congregation to the impact of Promise Keepers. "I feel that our church is in a different place. Our men are now ready to cross barriers and go into communities that if I had wanted our church to go into seven years ago, my action would have caused them to remove me a long time ago."

As an offshoot of this desire, Pastor Wooten and Pastor Arthur Johnson of Doers of the Word Church have nurtured a relationship that continues to encourage both pastors to live out their commitment to racial reconciliation. "He and I have stoked the vision of our churches and lives. It has fostered my facilitating his doing ministry. Since he can reach his community a lot better than we can, we have committed to equip them and support them to facilitate their ministry." In a bold step toward accomplishing that goal, New Life Assembly of God gives a tenth of its freewill offerings to help Doers of the Word.

NOTES

CHAPTER 1: *SEPARATE AND UNCONCERNED*

1. Benjamin Quarles, *The Negro in the Making of America* (New York: Simon & Schuster, 1996), 42. In the Colonial period many Africans did hold on to their African religious beliefs, but many converted to Christianity. As Eugene Genovese states, "From the moment the Africans lost the social basis of their religious community life, their religion itself had to disintegrate as a coherent system of belief. From the moment they arrived in America and began to toil as slaves, they could not help absorbing the religion of the master class. But, the conditions of their new social life forced them to combine their African inheritance with the dominant power they confronted and to shape a religion of their own. *In time they would produce a religion—or perhaps it would be better to say a sensibility on which a religious system could be built—that would help shape the mainstream of American Christianity and yet retain its special aspect as a black cultural expression.*" *Roll, Jordan, Roll: The World the Slaves Made* (New York: Vintage Books, 1976), 184; italics mine.

2. H. Shelton Smith, *In His Image, But . . . Racism in Southern Religion, 1780–1910* (Durham, N.C.: Duke University Press, 1972), 1.

3. John Hurd, *The Law of Freedom & Bondage in the United States,* vol. 1 (Boston: Little, Brown & Company, 1858), 236–37. Similar racially biased laws were also operating in other colonies (see pages 249–50, 263, 290, 292).

4. William Julius Wilson, *The Declining Significance of Race* (Chicago: University of Chicago Press, 1980), 28; Edmund S. Morgan, *American Slavery, American Freedom: The Ordeal of Colonial Virginia* (New York: W. W. Norton, 1975), 311.

5. Wilson, *The Declining Significance of Race,* 29.

6. Mary Stroughton Locke, *Anti-Slavery in America, from the Introduction of African Slaves to the Prohibition of the Slave Trade, 1619–1808,* Radcliffe College Monographs, no. II (Boston: Ginn & Company, 1901), 2–3. Philadelphia's Quaker merchants in the first third of the century were actively engaged in selling West Indian blacks. Some of these merchants continued in this trade up to the 1750s. See Smith, *In His Image,* 6.

7. Locke, *Anti-Slavery in America,* 13.

8. Ibid., 13–14.

9. My use of this phrase "living tools" is taken from Aristotle's description of slaves in ancient times. This appears in John Stott's *The Message of Ephesians* (Downers Grove, Ill.: InterVarsity Press, 1979), 251.

Although slavery is not identifed with the North as much as it is with the South, there is clear indication that it flourished in the North. Slaves in the North labored on farms, loaded and emptied ships, and built the infrastructure of many cities. The brutality that these slave laborers endured has recently been discovered in the excavation of a mass burial site for twenty thousand slaves from the 1700s in lower Manhattan. The skeletons found showed clear signs that they were "worked beyond the margins of physical capacity, especially undernourished children." "Only Remember Us: Skeletons of Slaves from New York Grave Bear Witness," *U.S. News & World Report* 123 (July 1997): 51–54.

10. Morgan, *American Slavery, American Freedom,* 312–13.

11. A major concern for masters was that the baptism of a slave would require that slave's master to free the slave. In fact the question had been settled earlier by legislative action. "In 1667 Virginia flatly declared 'that conferring of baptisme doth not alter the condition of the person as to his bondage or freedome.'" Smith, *In His Image,* 10, 11; see also Carter G. Woodson, *The Education of the Negro Prior to 1861* (New York: Arno Press and New York Times, 1968), 4.

12. Frank J. Klingberg, *Anglican Humanitarianism in Colonial New York* (Philadelphia: The Church Historical Society, 1940), 208, 209.

13. Samuel Sewall, *The Selling of Joseph: A Memorial,* ed. Sidney Kaplan (Cambridge: University of Massachusetts Press, 1969), 16–17.

14. Smith, *In His Image,* 165.

15. Locke, *Anti-Slavery in America,* 19.

16. Lorenzo Greene, *The Negro in Colonial New England, 1620–1776* (New York: Columbia University Press, 1942), 84.

17. Stuart C. Henry, *George Whitefield: Wayfaring Witness* (New York: Abingdon Press, 1957), 116.

18. Ibid., 117.

19. Ibid.

20. John Gillies, *Memoirs of the Life of the Reverend George Whitefield* (New Haven: Andrus & Starr, 1812), 222; see also Henry, *George Whitefield,* 117.

21. Smith, *In His Image,* 38–40.

22. James O'Kelly, *Essay on Negro Slavery* (Philadelphia: Prentice Hall, 1789), 10.

Notes

23. John Hope Franklin, "The Moral Legacy of the Founding Fathers," in *Race and History: Selected Essays 1938–1988* (Baton Rouge: Louisiana State University Press, 1989), 161; italics his.

24. Edward Peeks, *The Long Struggle for Black Power* (New York: Charles Scribner's Sons, 1971), 16; Maria Mallory, "See How Far We Have Come," *U.S. News & World Report* 123 (November 1997): 10; Eric Lincoln and Lawrence Mamiya, *The Black Church in the African American Experience* (Durham, N.C.: Duke University Press, 1990), 51.

25. *Negro Population, 1790–1915* (Department of Commerce, Bureau of the Census, Washington, 1918), 57. Also Smith, *In His Image*, 74.

26. During the 1800s many of the letters, private diaries, and journals of slaveholders evidenced sincere religious feelings for their slaves. George DeBerniere Hooper of Alabama referred to the loss of a slave as not only the loss of a "friend" but also of a "Brother in Christ." Ebenezer Jones of Tennessee wrote to his children:

Dear son and daughter may you ever mind
And to your slaves be always very kind
You soon with them on a level must meet
When Christ doth call you to his judgment seat
Christ will not ask if folks are black or white
But judge the deeds and pass a sentence right
The earth is not a place for our abode
Prepare, prepare to meet a righteous God.
Genovese, *Roll, Jordan, Roll,* 190, 191.

27. John Blassingame, *The Slave Community: Plantation Life in the Antebellum South* (New York: Oxford University Press, 1972), 60; Moses Roper, *A Narrative of the Adventures and Escape of Moses Roper from American Slavery* (Philadelphia: Merrihew & Gunn, 1838), 51.

28. Blassingame, *The Slave Community,* 62.

29. A good example of this is a slave woman who had to be excluded from a Baptist church in Kentucky in 1807 because, on becoming a Christian, she denounced slavery. She had the seemingly wild idea that no Christian should own slaves. Genovese, *Roll, Jordan, Roll,* 192.

30. Lunsford Lane, "The Narratives of Lunsford Lane," in *Five Slave Narratives,* ed. William Loren Katz (New York: Arno Press and New York Times, 1968), 21.

31. David Chesebrough notes that the failure of the Christian clergy was not only in what they said but also in what they failed to say. "The churches chose to place their emphasis upon individual responsibility and 'spiritual' matters, and neglected to speak to the great social ills of the day." *God Ordained This War: Sermons on the Sectional Crisis, 1830–1865,* ed. David B. Chesebrough (Columbia, S.C.: University of South Carolina Press, 1991), 3.

32. Smith, *In His Image,* 34.

33. Ibid., 35–36.

34. Ibid., 74, 76.

35. Lawrence Thomas Lesick, *The Lane Rebels: Evangelicalism and Anti-slavery in Antebellum America* (Methchen, N.J.: The Scarecrow Press, 1980), 84, 108–9. Charles Cole strongly states, "No one was more influential, directly or indirectly, in winning converts to abolitionsim than the Oberlin evangelist." Charles C. Cole Jr., *The Social Ideas of the Northern Evangelists 1826–1860* (New York: Columbia University Press, 1954), 204.

36. Ibid., 176–80.

37. The growing openness of the slaveholders in the 1800s to the spiritual needs of the slaves caused great turmoil for many ministers who had to select a position on slavery that would accomplish the greatest result through the highest means. Genovese highlights the southern clergy's failure in stating, "The clergy faced a choice. Should it follow the example of the Quakers or of other small groups and take high ground against slavery? If so, it would be rendered, perhaps with no small amount of violence, irrelevant to the lives of the slaves. Or should it place the souls of the slaves above all material considerations and render unto Caesar the things which are Caesar's? The troublemakers were dealt with, and the deed was done. Step by step, the several churches embraced the proslavery argument. They won the trust of the masters and freed themselves to preach the gospel to the slaves."

The general assembly of the Presbyterian Church adopted this position. They declared in 1861 that the slave system had generally proven "kindly and benevolent" and had provided "real effective discipline" to a people who could not be elevated in any other way. It concluded that slavery was the black man's "normal condition." The Alabama Baptist Association at its annual meeting in 1850 called for greater efforts to instruct the slaves by noting the benefit to slaveholders. "Intelligent masters with the light of experience before them will regard the communication of sound religious instruction as the truest economy and the most efficient police and as tending to the greatest utility, with regard to every interest involved." Genovese, *Roll, Jordan, Roll,* 187, 189.

38. James Gillespie Birney, *The American Churches: The Bulwarks of American Slavery* (New York: Arno Press and New York Times, 1842), 6–8.

39. Philo Tower, *Slavery Unmasked: Being a Truthful Narrative of a Three Years' Residence and Journeys in Eleven Southern States: To Which Is Added the Invasion of Kansas, including the Last Chapter of Her Wrongs* (New York: Negro Universities Press, 1856), 393; italics his.

40. Albert Barnes, *The Church and Slavery* (1857; New York: Negro Universities Press, 1969), 22. In a very sharp statement on the nature of the church and its work in society, Barnes states, "Slavery touches on society at a thousand different points; and it is impossible that there should be *any* institution in a region where slavery prevails which will not be more or less affected by it. Besides, though the churches located in the midst of slavery may be wholly free from any direct participation in it, it is still true

that the church is designed to influence all surrounding institutions. This is a part of its mission in the world,—a part of the reason why it is established and perpetuated on the earth. The church often springs up in the midst of a mass of moral corruption for the very purpose of modifying by its influence existing institutions, and changing the whole aspect of society. Pure in itself, it sheds a benign influence on all around, and its contact with prevailing institutions rebukes what is wrong and suggests and sanctions what is right. By a healthful contact it diffuses moral purity through a community. A church, therefore, located in the midst of slavery, though all its members may be wholly unconnected with slavery, yet owes an important duty to society and to God in reference to the system; and its mission will not be accomplished by securing merely the sanctification of its own members, or even by drawing within its fold multitudes of those who shall be saved" (pp. 20–22).

41. C. Bruce Staiger, "Abolitionism and the Presbyterian Schism of 1837–1838," *Mississippi Valley Historical Review* XXXVI (December 1949): 392.

42. Charles Hodge, "Slavery," *Biblical Repertory* 8 (April 1836): 268–305. Hodge's position can be summed up in his statement, "We see no way of escape from the conclusion that the conduct of the modern abolitionists, being directly opposed to that of the authors of our religion, must be wrong and ought to be modified or abandoned" (p. 277).

43. Locke, *Anti-Slavery in America,* 44; Birney, *The American Churches,* 21, 23.

44. "Reply of the Acting Board, December 17th, 1844," *Baptist Missionary Magazine* XXV (August 1845): 222; see also Chesebrough, *God Ordained This War,* 194; Smith, *In His Image,* 126.

45. Chesebrough, *God Ordained This War,* 193.

46. Ibid., 143, 145–50.

CHAPTER 2: *SEPARATE AND UNINVOLVED*

1. Booker T. Washington, who was a young slave at this time, compares emancipation to the sending of a ten- or twelve-year-old child into the world to provide food and shelter for himself and his children, to educate himself and others, and to provide for the establishment and support of churches. *Up from Slavery: An Autobiography* (New York: A. L. Burt Company, 1901), 21–22.

2. My use of the term *segregation* refers to the physical separation of people on the basis of race. The extreme nature of separation on the basis of race in the United States rivals similar attempts in India and South Africa, as historical examples reveal. South Carolina created separate schools for mulatto children, white children, and black children. Jim Crow Bibles were discovered for black court witnesses in Atlanta. One of the most extreme examples of this separation, though, is the fact that North Carolina and Florida required the textbooks that were used by black children in the public schools to be kept separate from the books that were

used by white children. The Florida law even stipulated that these books had to be separated while they were in storage. C. Vann Woodward, *The Strange Career of Jim Crow* (New York: Oxford University Press, 1966), 102.

3. The Supreme Court's ruling in the *Plessy v. Ferguson* case had clear signs of racism. This is evident in Justice Henry B. Brown's writing for the 8–1 majority that agreed that Homer Adolph Plessy had no business sitting in the white section of a Louisiana train. Brown stated, "If one race be inferior to the other socially, the Constitution of the United States cannot put them on the same plane." This decision provided a legal basis for segregated train cars and for the next fifty-eight years of Jim Crow's "separate but equal" discrimination in the South. See Ellis Cose, "The Realities of Black and White: Jim Crow Is Long Dead, but the Promise of Integration Remains Unfulfilled," *Newsweek* 127 (April 1996): 36.

4. It is unfortunate but the Ku Klux Klan came to be recognized as a part of southern Christianity because many religious southerners erroneously viewed it as a movement to restore morality and Christian values during Reconstruction. A primary example of this evaluation of the Klan is the story behind the 1915 motion picture epic *The Birth of a Nation*. Although the first Klan was dissolved in 1869, the seeds of its resurgence were planted by the Reverend Thomas Dixon Jr., who romanticized the Klan's significance in his novel *The Clansman*. This novel was later made into the movie *The Birth of a Nation* by another southerner, D. W. Griffith, who was also the son of an ex-Confederate officer.

The movie depicts the Klan as the savior of the South from savage, recently freed blacks during Reconstruction. Its first showings in New York and Boston brought protest until Rev. Dixon removed opposition by having his old classmate and then president, Woodrow Wilson, his cabinet, and their families view the film. After seeing the movie, the southern-born president said that it was like "writing history with lightning . . . my only regret is that it is all so terribly true."

The movie was so moving and influential that it led to the rebirth of a second Ku Klux Klan in 1915, which would later reach a membership high of five million in the mid-1920s. Even today the movie continues to be one of the most powerful recruiting tools of the Klan. Charles Reagan Wilson, *Baptized in Blood: The Religion of the Lost Cause 1865–1920* (Athens, Ga.: University of Georgia Press, 1980), 112–16; "Birth of a Nation," *Klanwatch Intelligence Report* (Southern Poverty Law Center, 1981), 18; Derrick Bell, "Racial Imperative in American Law," in *The Age of Segregation: Race Relations in the South, 1890–1945,* ed. Robert Haws (Jackson, Miss.: University Press of Mississippi, 1978), 11, 135.

Blacks in this same Reconstruction period, such as Booker T. Washington, had a different view of the Klan. Washington states that the Klan operated mainly at night and their main objective was to quash the political aspirations of Negroes, and part of this strategy led them to burn the schoolhouses and churches of blacks. He states that the Ku Klux Klan period was the darkest part of the overall Reconstruction period. *Up from Slavery,* 78.

5. Much of the violence of this period, that was not mindless, sought to intimidate blacks who voted or tried to become involved in politics. This is evident in the fact that blacks were seldom lynched in the slavery period. It is estimated that only 10 percent of the three hundred lynching victims from 1840 to 1860 were black, but in the last sixteen years of the 1800s the majority of the twenty-five hundred lynching victims were black. The fear of quick and uncontrolled violence and even rumors of atrocities committed against blacks, especially when political elections were near, had a powerful effect on safeguarding white power in society. Wilson, *The Declining Significance of Race,* 59; Mary Frances Berry, "Repression of Blacks in the South 1890–1945: Enforcing the System of Segregation," in *The Age of Segregation,* ed. Haws, 41.

6. Wilson, *Baptized in Blood,* 101.

7. D. W. Stowell, *Rebuilding Zion: The Religious Reconstruction of the South, 1863–1877* (New York: Oxford University Press, 1998), 85; Ted Ownby, *Subduing Satan: Religion, Recreation, and Manhood in the Rural South, 1865–1920* (Chapel Hill, N.C.: University of North Carolina Press, 1990), 137.

8. Lincoln and Mamiya, *The Black Church in the African American Experience,* 28, 31, 46, 48.

9. The position of the church as a key place for interracial contacts is noted in this 1956 quote by Dr. Frank T. Wilson, an African American theologian and dean of Howard University's School of Religion, as he discussed the great difficulty churches face in achieving racial integration. "Worshipping together is a more personal thing than riding trains or attending movies together. Tolerance is not enough; it must be real brotherhood or nothing." Lee Nichols and Louis Cassels, "The Churches Repent," *Reader's Digest* 68 (February 1956): 62–66.

10. Berry, "Repression of Blacks in the South 1890–1945," 39.

11. Josiah Strong, *Our Country* (1885; reprint, Cambridge, Mass.: The Belknap Press of Harvard University Press, 1963), 215–16.

12. Gilbert Osofsky, *Harlem: The Making of a Ghetto, Negro New York, 1890–1930* (New York: Harper Torchbooks, 1971), 41–42.

13. "11 Negroes Attend Blackshear Service: Pastor Avoids Direct Mention of Race—Six Detectives at Brooklyn Church," *New York Times* LXXIX (September 1929): 36. David Morgan Reimers, "Protestant Churches and the Negro: A Study of Several Major Protestant Denominations and the Negro from World War One to 1954" (Ph.D. diss., University of Wisconsin, 1961), 62–63.

14. We must note, unfortunately, that even in the inception of this movement the racism of American culture influenced and shaped the movement's leaders. One article states that Charles Parham, a white leader who has been recognized as the "father of American Pentecostalism," worked with Seymour but continued to endorse the Ku Klux Klan as late

as 1927. See J. Lee Grady, "Pentecostals Renounce Racism," *Christianity Today* 38 (December 1994): 58; David D. Daniels, "They Had a Dream: Racial Harmony Broke Down, but the Hope Did Not," *Christian History* 17 (spring 1998): 19–21.

15. The Holiness movement was originally a reform movement within Methodism and dates back to 1867. Holiness churches split from Methodism in the 1890s as the differences became increasingly more contentious. The Holiness movement included blacks and whites who were drawn to the Azusa Street revival in Los Angeles. See Lincoln and Mamiya, *The Black Church in the African American Experience,* 78–79, 81; James S. Tinney, "Black Origins of the Pentecostal Movement," *Christianity Today* 16 (October 1971): 4–6.

16. In the summer of 1919, immediately following the end of World War I, decorated black soldiers came home to find the enemy of racial hatred far greater than what they had experienced in Europe. Race suppression in urban areas, lynchings, and even war veterans being burned alive while wearing their uniforms occurred during this "red" summer and throughout the period of Mason's ministry. See Reimers, "Protestant Churches and the Negro," 4; Lincoln and Mamiya, *The Black Church in the African American Experience,* 82–83. Historian John Hope Franklin called this summer the "greatest period of interracial strife the nation had ever witnessed." *From Slavery to Freedom: A History of Negro Americans* (New York: Knopf, 1967), 480.

17. Frank Samuel Loescher, *The Protestant Church and the Negro: A Pattern of Segregation* (Westport, Conn.: Negro Universities Press, 1971), 15, 77, 144–46.

18. Reimers, "Protestant Churches and the Negro," 306.

19. Joyce Hollyday, "The Dream That Has Endured: Clarence Jordan and Koinonia," *Sojourners* 8 (December 1979), 12.

20. Jordan's good friend Dr. G. McLeod Bryan, while reminiscing about his friend, said, "Unlike many of the professional theologians, Clarence did not disdain the local church. Yet, paradoxically, he is perhaps the only one of his rank to be expelled from his local church (expelled incidentally, not for being less moral than the congregation, but for being more moral)." G. McLeod Bryan, "Theology in Overalls: The Imprint of Clarence Jordan" *Sojourners* 8 (December 1979), 11.

21. Hollyday, "The Dream That Has Endured," 12–18; Clarence Jordan and Bill Land Doulos, *Cotton Patch Parables of Liberation* (Scottdale, Pa.: Herald Press, 1976); Bryan, "Theology in Overalls: The Imprint of Clarence Jordan," 10–11.

CHAPTER 3: *SEPARATE AND ALARMED*

1. The high court's decision was viewed as such a debilitating blow to southern segregation that four states (Louisiana, Mississippi, North Carolina, and Georgia) imposed sanctions and penalties against compliance with the Supreme Court's decision. Georgia went as far as making it a

felony for any school official of the state, or any municipal or county schools, to spend tax money for public schools in which the races were integrated. Across Mississippi the day of the decision was called "black Monday." Soon citizens' councils, comprised of white community leaders, across the state were working to keep the white race from being defiled through integration. These councils began offering cash prizes to high school students with the best essays promoting segregation. For third graders the councils recommended that they learn to read using these lines: "Negroes use their own bathrooms. They do not use white people's bathrooms. . . . This is called our Southern Way of Life." Woodward, *The Strange Career of Jim Crow*, 150–53, 157; see also Lewis Lord, "Painful Secrets from the Defiant Years," *U.S. News & World Report* 124 (March 1998): 30.

2. Cose, "The Realities of Black and White," 36; Reimers, "Protestant Churches and the Negro," iv.

3. Jeannye Thornton, "'I'm Not Going to Ride the Bus': Forty Years Ago, Ordinary People Made History," *U.S. News & World Report* 119 (December 1995): 52–54.

4. During these years black comedian Dick Gregory noted that the North was as racist as the South: "the system of oppression over black people does not begin south of the Mason-Dixon line. It really begins south of the Canadian border." Dick Gregory, *The Shadow That Scares Me*, ed. James R. McGraw (New York: Pocket Books, 1969), 32.

5. Jody Miller Shearer, "Mennonites and Racism: Much Work to Do," *The Mennonite* 112 (January 1997): 3.

6. Nichols and Cassels, "The Churches Repent," 63.

7. Edward Gilbreath, "The 'Jackie Robinson' of Evangelism," *Christianity Today* 42 (February 1998): 55.

8. The prophecy of the activists would prove to be accurate. The Kerner Commission, appointed by President Johnson to determine why the northern riots occurred and how they could be prevented from occurring again, reported in 1968 that "our nation is moving toward two societies, one black, one white—separate and unequal," and then stated, "what white Americans have never fully understood—but what the Negro can never forget—is that white society is deeply implicated in the ghetto. White institutions created it, white institutions maintain it, and white society condones it." Henry Hampton and Steve Fayer, *Voices of Freedom: An Oral History of the Civil Rights Movement from the 1950s through the 1980s* (New York: Bantam Books, 1990), 398.

9. Stokely Carmichael and Charles V. Hamilton, *Black Power: The Politics of Liberation in America* (New York: Vintage Books, 1967), 44.

10. Alex Haley, *The Autobiography of Malcolm X* (New York: Ballantine Books, 1984), 200–201.

Notes

CHAPTER 4: *SEPARATE BUT EVANGELICAL*

1. Will Norton Jr., "An Interview with John Perkins, the Prophet," *Christianity Today* 26 (January 1982): 21.

2. Billy Graham, "Why Don't Our Churches Practice the Brotherhood They Preach?" *Reader's Digest* 72 (August 1960), 52–56. In this *Reader's Digest* article Graham boldly calls for both black and white Christians to take a stand: "If we cannot work together in a spiritual dimension, how can we expect citizens to do so on more secular levels? Though the race question has important social implications, it is fundamentally a moral and spiritual issue. Only moral and spiritual approaches can provide a solution" (p. 54). Graham's written challenge to the racial prejudice within Christianity initially appeared in his 1956 *Life* article "Billy Graham Makes a Plea for an End to Intolerance," *Life* 41 (October 1, 1956), 138–51.

3. W. A. Criswell, *Look Up, Brother!: The Buoyant Assertion of What's Right with Us* (Nashville: Broadman, 1970), 50; Joe Maxwell, "Black Southern Baptists: The SBC's Valiant Efforts to Overcome Its Racist Past," *Christianity Today* 39 (May 1995): 28.

4. Bob Jones III in a 1978 federal trial testified that the school's beliefs are based on the Bible, which teaches that three races descended from Noah's three sons. He also stated, "God has divided people religiously; he has divided them geographically; he has divided them racially. But there is coming a day when all of that will cease, and until that day comes, we intend to do our best to keep the lines that God has established." Beth Spring, "The Ominous Implications of the Bob Jones Decision," *Christianity Today* 27 (July 1983): 26.

5. In defending the university's position on the *Larry King Live* show, university president Bob Jones III argued that the school's position on interracial marriages and dating was based on their desire to not support the world system of the coming Antichrist. "People think we don't let them date because we are racist. In other words to be racist you have to treat people differently. We don't. We don't let them date, because we were trying, as an example, to enforce something, a principle that is much greater than this. We stand against the one-world government, against the coming world of Anitchrist, which is a one-world system of blending, of all differences, of blending of national differences, economic differences, church differences, into a big one ecumenical world. The Bible is very clear about this. We said, you know, way back years ago, when we first had a problem, which was—by the way, we started this principle back in the mid-'50s. I was a college student at BJU at the time and it was with an Asian and Caucasian—we didn't even have black students for another fifteen years. So it was not put there as a black thing. I think people need to understand that." Taken from the transcripts of the *Larry King Live* show, which was aired March 3, 2000.

The university's Web site justified the university's policy by stating, "Does the University believe that those who choose interracial marriage do so out of rebellion against God? No. It does believe, however, that often the *promoters* of it do so out of antagonism toward God because they are often the same entities that promote homosexuality, abortion, and other forms of social radicalism. Bob Jones University's policy regarding interracial dating was more of an opposition to the rebellious and defiant Antichrist spirit of the promoters of one-worldism than to interracial dating itself. Many who date and marry interracially are just as opposed to one-worldism and the spirit of Antichrist as we are." "The Truth about Bob Jones University" on the Web at www.bju.edu/fresponse.html.

6. Beth Spring, "Falwell Raises a Stir by Opposing Sanctions against South Africa," *Christianity Today* 29 (October 1985): 53.

7. Vincent N. Parillo, *Strangers to These Shores: Race and Ethnic Relations in the United States* (Needham Heights, Mass.: Simon & Schuster, 1997), 365; Brian Duffy, "Days of Rage," *U.S. News & World Report* 112 (May 1992): 21–26.

8. Joe B. Feagin and Clarice B. Feagin, *Racial and Ethnic Relations* (Upper Saddle River, N.J.: Prentice Hall, 1999): 250; John Farley, *Majority-Minority Relations* (Englewood Cliffs, N.J.: Prentice Hall, 1995): 179–80.

9. Timothy C. Morgan, "Racial Reconciliation: Simpson Verdict, Farrakhan March Energize Interracial Dialogue," *Christianity Today* 39 (November 1995): 78.

10. Bill McCartney, "A Call to Unity," in *Seven Promises of a Promise Keeper* (Colorado Springs, Colorado: Focus on the Family Publishing, 1994), 160.

11. Hiawatha Bray, "Evangelical Racism," *Christianity Today* 36 (November 1992): 42.

12. Ibid., 44.

13. Andres Tapia, "The Myth of Racial Progress," *Christianity Today* 37 (October 1993): 18.

14. Ibid.

15. Billy Graham, "Racism and the Evangelical Church," *Christianity Today* 37 (October 1993): 27.

16. J. Lee Grady, "Pentecostals Renounce Racism," *Christianity Today* 38 (December 1994): 58.

17. Timothy C. Morgan, "Racist No More? Black Leaders Ask," *Christianity Today* 39 (August 1995): 53.

18. Maxwell, "Black Southern Baptists: The SBC's Valiant Efforts to Overcome Its Racist Past," 26–31.

19. Edward Gilbreath, "Catching Up with a Dream: Evangelicals and Race 30 Years after the Death of Martin Luther King, Jr.," *Christianity Today* 42 (March 1998): 28.

CHAPTER 5: *STILL SEPARATE*

1. Paula Span, "Casting of Black Jesus Incites Tumult," *Raleigh, N.C. News & Observer* 7 March 1997, 9A.

Notes

CHAPTER 6: *RACE IN THE BIBLE*

1. Robert Creamer, *Babe* (New York: Penguin Books, 1988), 38.
2. Feagin and Feagin, *Racial and Ethnic Relations,* 5.

CHAPTER 7: *THE MISSING LINK*

1. F. F. Bruce, *The Epistles to the Colossians, to Philemon, and to the Ephesians* (Grand Rapids: Eerdmans, 1984); William Barclay, *The Letters to the Philippians, Colossians, and Thessalonians* (Philadelphia: Westminster Press, 1975), 154–56.
2. F. F. Bruce commenting on Colossians 3:11 states, "Natural and racial idiosyncrasies may survive, but in such a way as to contribute to the living variety of the people of Christ, not so as to create or perpetuate any difference in spiritual status." *The Epistles to the Colossians, to Philemon, and to the Ephesians,* 149.
3. Michael Green, *Evangelism through the Local Church: A Comprehensive Guide to All Aspects of Evangelism* (Nashville: Thomas Nelson, 1992), 33–34.
4. See Michael W. Apple, "On Analyzing Hegemony," *Journal of Curriculum Theorizing* 1 (1979): 10–43; Clifford Geertz, "The Entry into Meaning," *Readings: A Journal of Reviews and Commentary in Mental Health* 12 (1997): 6–9; and Jerome S. Bruner, *The Culture of Education* (Cambridge, Mass.: Harvard University Press, 1996).
5. Stephen Charles Mott, *Biblical Ethics and Social Change* (New York: Oxford University Press, 1982), 6.
6. This figure can also be applied to sanctification. We are positionally justified and positionally sanctified in Christ, but we are responsible to now strive to make our positional reality our experiential reality.
7. Donald W. Burdick, "James," in *The Expositor's Bible Commentary,* vol. 12, gen. ed. Frank E. Gaebelein (Grand Rapids: Zondervan, 1981), 182.
8. "We Are Giving Them Back Their Culture: An Interview with Rachel Saint," *Christianity Today* 20 (January 1976): 14–16.
9. Lesslie Newbigin, *The Gospel in a Pluralist Society* (Grand Rapids: Eerdmans, 1991), 227.

CHAPTER 8: *THE PROOFS IN THE PATTERN*

1. R. E. O. White, "Reconciliation," in *Evangelical Dictionary of Theology,* ed. Walter A. Elwell (Grand Rapids: Baker, 1984), 917.
2. Craig Keener has given this event the amusing label, "How to have a Christian riot." "The Gospel and Racial Reconciliation," in *The Gospel in Black and White: Theological Resources for Racial Reconciliation,* ed. Dennis L. Okholm (Downers Grove, Ill.: InterVarsity Press, 1997), 120.

CHAPTER 9: *THE RECONCILIATION CONTINUUM*

1. A *Life* magazine centerfold shows Temple Baptist's five thousand Sunday school attendees standing in front of the church building with the

caption "what is probably the biggest Sunday School group picture ever taken." *Life* 40 (December 1955): 54.

2. "Countdown to Crisis in Plains," *Christianity Today* 21 (December 1976): 50.

3. Manuel Ortiz, *One New People: Models for Developing a Multiethnic Church* (Downers Grove, Ill.: InterVarsity Press, 1996), 66–68.

4. Martin Luther King Jr., "The Ethical Demands for Integration," in *A Testament of Hope: The Essential Writings and Speeches of Martin Luther King, Jr.,* ed. James M. Washington (San Francisco: HarperCollins, 1986), 118.

5. A firsthand description of the division that developed within Circle Church is presented by Glen Kehrein in Raleigh Washington and Glen Kehrein, *Breaking Down Walls: A Model for Reconciliation in an Age of Racial Strife* (Chicago: Moody, 1993). The watershed issues are presented in Clarence Hilliard's "Down with the Honky Christ—Up with the Funky Jesus," *Christianity Today* 20 (January 1976): 6–8. An excellent critique of the church is also offered by Manuel Ortiz, "Circle Church: A Case Study in Contextualization," *Urban Missions* 8 (January, 1991), 6–18.

6. Susan Kauffman, "'Change Hearts by Changing Heads': Noted Historian Gives Views on Racial Issues," *Raleigh, N.C. News & Observer,* 3 September 1997, 4B.

7. Ortiz, *One New People,* 72–85.

CHAPTER 10: *THE BUCK STOPS HERE*

1. Jim Cymbala with Dean Merrill, *Fresh Wind, Fresh Fire: What Happens When Real Faith Ignites God's People* (Grand Rapids: Zondervan, 1997), 72.

2. To obtain more details on the "Breakfast Club" program, contact the Chicago Urban Reconciliation Enterprise, P.O. Box 804113, Chicago, IL 60680-4103, or phone (773) 374-4330.

3. Robert E. Webber, *Blended Worship: Achieving Substance and Relevance in Worship* (Peabody, Mass.: Hendrickson Publishers, 1998), 66.

4. John Stott, *Our Social and Sexual Revolution: Major Issues for a New Century,* rev. ed. (Grand Rapids: Baker, 1999), 78.

CHAPTER 11: *ALL FOR ONE*

1. Washington and Kehrein, *Breaking Down Walls,* 130–33.

2. "Whether the label is deserved or undeserved, in the minds of most blacks, all white people are 'white folks' until they prove themselves 'different.' It is part life experience, part self-preservation, and part projection. I have questioned very intelligent black people who admit that this 'sizing up' of whites is often not very objective. But it takes place just the same." Spencer Perkins, "Playing the Grace Card," *Christianity Today* 42 (July 1998): 42.

3. For a good discussion of white Americans' response to slavery see Gordon Marino, "Me? Apologize for Slavery?" *Christianity Today* 42 (October 1998): 82–83.

4. Washington, *Up from Slavery,* 165.

5. Mike Tharp, "Fringe Groups and Y2K: A Scary Mix," *U.S. News & World Report* 127 (6 September 1999): 58.

6. Martin Luther King Jr., *Why We Can't Wait* (New York: Penguin Books, 1964), 88–89.

SUGGESTED READING

A Historical Overview of African American Contributions in America

Bennett, Lerone, Jr. *Before the Mayflower: A History of Black America.* New York: Penguin Books, 1982. Bennett's book traces black history from its roots in Africa but primarily focuses on the contributions of Africans in America.

DuBois, William E. B. *The Souls of Black Folk.* New York: American Library, 1969. This is a compilation of beautifully written essays examining the aspirations and experiences of African Americans at the turn of the twentieth century. Although dated, you will gain cultural and historical insights.

Haley, Alex. *The Autobiography of Malcolm X.* New York: Ballantine Books, 1984. This book will give you an understanding of the impact of American racism in the lives of African Americans, as it is expressed through the eyes of a modern symbol of black strength and self-determination.

Quarles, Benjamin. *The Negro in the Making of America.* New York: Simon & Schuster, 1996. This book will give you a good historical overview of the contributions of African Americans in the United States.

History of Black Christians in America

Ellis, Carl F., Jr. *Free at Last?: The Gospel in the African-American Experience.* Downers Grove, Ill.: InterVarsity Press, 1996. This book will give the reader a thoughtful overview of African-American culture and the role the gospel has played and continues to play within this culture.

Lincoln, C. Eric, and Lawrence Mamiya. *The Black Church in the African American Experience.* Durham, N. C.: Duke University Press, 1990. This comprehensive work will give you great insight into the origins and nature of the various denominations that make up the Black Church in America.

Usry, Glenn, and Craig S. Keener. *Black Man's Religion: Can Christianity Be Afro-centric?* Downers Grove, Ill.: InterVarsity Press, 1996. *Black Man's Religion* shows the reader the important contributions African Americans have made to Christianity and is a good counterbalance to the depiction of Christianity as a "white" religion.

Tools for Racial Reconciliation

For an Interpersonal Ministry

DeYoung, Curtiss Paul. *Coming Together: The Bible's Message in an Age of Diversity.* Valley Forge, Pa.: Judson Press, 1995. *Coming Together* is a well thought out consideration and argument for the importance of the ministry of racial reconciliation to the American church.

Evans, Tony. *Let's Get to Know Each Other: What White and Black Christians Need to Know about Each Other.* Nashville: Thomas Nelson, 1995. This book addresses many of the issues separating black and white Christians thereby preparing the reader for many of the perspective issues that will be encountered in an interpersonal ministry of reconciliation.

Perkins, Spencer, and Chris Rice. *More than Equals: Racial Healing for the Sake of the Gospel.* Downers Grove, Ill.: InterVarsity Press, 1993. Here are the personal insights of two close friends from different racial backgrounds on the topic of racial reconciliation. Their suggestions are practical and honest as they argue the need for racial harmony.

For a Church-Based Ministry

Breckenridge, James and Lillian. *What Color Is Your God?: Multicultural Education in the Church.* Wheaton, Ill.: Victor Press, 1995. Note that this is a textbook but it does present information that becomes a solid foundation for the establishment of a multicultural ministry in any church.

Ortiz, Manuel. *One New People: Models for Developing a Multiethnic Church.* Downers Grove, Ill.: InterVarsity Press, 1996. Using a workbook format, this book provides various ideas, questions, and models to assist in the process of implementing or expanding a church's multiracial ministry.

Washington, Raleigh, and Glen Kehrein. *Breaking Down Walls: A Model for Reconciliation in an Age of Racial Strife.* Chicago: Moody Press, 1993. This book presents a very honest and personal look at the challenges of personal and church racial reconciliation through the lenses of two men who have forged a friendship and ministry across racial lines. The strengths of this work are its practical insights and the ministry mode the authors present.

Washington, Raleigh, Glen Kehrein, and Claude V. King. *Breaking Down the Walls: Experiencing Biblical Reconciliation and Unity in the Body of Christ.* Chicago: Moody Press, 1997. A very practical and interactive workbook that includes detailed lessons, study questions, Scripture memorization cards, a list of resources, and activity guides to be used in a church.

Theological Basis for Racial Reconciliation

Mott, Stephen Charles. *Biblical Ethics and Social Change.* New York: Oxford University Press, 1982. This is a scholarly work that wonderfully constructs a justification on the basis of Christian social ethics for the church's identity as counterculture.

Okholm, Dennis L., ed. *The Gospel in Black and White: Theological Resources for Racial Reconciliation.* Downers Grove, Ill.: InterVarsity Press, 1997. This is a compilation of various essays by a diverse group of theologians and pastors that gives a solid foundation for the importance of the ministry of racial reconciliation. A source of good preaching and teaching material.

Norman A. Peart is a sociologist and pastor who received his Ph.D. from Michigan State University and his master of divinity and master of theology degrees from Grand Rapids Baptist Seminary. He is the founding pastor of Grace Bible Fellowship, a multiracial church in Cary, North Carolina. He is also the founder of Grace Ministries. Norm, his wife, Carolyn, and their four sons live in Cary.